THE IMPOSSIBLE DREAMERS

SEARCH FOR AMELIA EARHART

BY

REBECCA PRICE JANNEY

Multnomah Publishers • Sisters, Oregon

SEARCH FOR AMELIA EARHART
published by Multnomah Fiction
a division of Multnomah Publishers, Inc.

© 1997 by Rebecca Price Janney
International Standard Book Number: 1-57673-026-3

Cover illustration by Tony Meers
Design by D^2 DesignWorks

Printed in the United States of America

For information:
MULTNOMAH PUBLISHERS, INC.
POST OFFICE BOX 1720
SISTERS, OREGON 97759

Library of Congress Cataloging-in-Publication Data:
Janney, Rebecca Price, 1957- Search for Amelia Earhart/Rebecca Price
Janney. p. cm.–(Impossible dreamers series; bk. 3) Summary: While talk-
ing about Amelia Earhart during their flight to Hawaii, a group of
Christian home school students and their tutor travel back to the time of
this famous aviator. ISBN 1-57673-026-3 (alk. paper) 1. Earhart,
Amelia, 1897-1937–Juvenile fiction. [1. Earhart, Amelia, 1897-1937–
Fiction. 2. Time travel–Fiction. 3. Christian life–Fiction.] I. Title. II.
Series: Janney, Rebecca Price, 1957-   Impossible dreamers series; bk. 3.
PZ7.J2433Se   1997   97-26592   [Fic]–dc21   CIP   AC
97 98 99 00 01 02 03 — 10 9 8 7 6 5 4 3 2 1

To Bill Myers,
with whom I've had adventures in writing.

AUTHOR'S NOTE

In addition to Amelia Earhart, many people in this book are historic figures, including Walter McMenamy, Bernard Baruch, G. P. Putnam, Paul Mantz, Mrs. Amy Earhart, and the DeCarries. Likewise, much of the activity surrounding Miss Earhart's historic flight is based on true accounts. I have, however, used creative license in describing these historic figures as well as taken an educated guess regarding what happened to Amelia Earhart after her disappearance. Her final words are strictly the product of my imagination.

Two books provided helpful material for me: *Lost Star* by Randall Brink and *Amelia Earhart* by Doris L. Rich.

Chapter One

"I just love it when the plane takes off!" Lindsey Skillman clapped her hands in delight and pressed her nose against the window.

"It's cool, all right." Her eleven-year-old brother, Andrew, leaned across her to watch as, beneath them, the city of San Francisco grew more and more distant.

Lindsey turned to glance at their cousin Ben in the aisle seat opposite them. "It'll be okay, Ben. We'll make it." Twelve-year-old Ben didn't like to fly. On the first leg of their trip, after they left their home in Virginia, he had gripped his armrests for an hour.

"I know. I keep repeating that Bible verse, 'I can do all things through Christ who strengthens me.'" He paused. "Even fly."

"Good idea!" At thirteen, Lindsey felt responsible for Andrew and Ben, even when their tutor was with them. "Isn't this great, T.J.?" she said, turning to him now.

But Thomas Jefferson Wakesnoris didn't share her joy either. In fact, he appeared more than a little green around the gills. Next to his reddish blond hair, T.J.'s skin was pale. He leaned his head back, moaned quietly, and clutched his airsick bag tightly.

The twenty-four-year-old tutor homeschooled Lindsey and the boys. Now he was escorting them to Hawaii, where they would join Lindsey's parents, who had flown there five days earlier for a professor's conference. Ben's mother would arrive in a couple days and they would all be on vacation for two whole weeks. Lindsey was so excited, she could hardly sit still.

She gazed through the slightly scratched window. Below her the Pacific Ocean ebbed and flowed. It was the first time she had ever seen it.

"The ocean is so gray! It looks almost harsh compared to the Atlantic." She turned to Andrew. "My ears just popped! Did yours?"

"Yeah. I hate that feeling."

"How about yours, T.J.?" she asked.

"Huh?" He leaned across Andrew, and Lindsey repeated herself.

"My ears are so stopped up I wish they'd pop more." T.J. smiled sheepishly. "I'm afraid I don't fly very well."

"You were okay when we left Virginia. You'll be fine in a few minutes." Lindsey patted his arm.

"At least I'm in good company."

Lindsey nodded. "Ben doesn't like this either."

"That's not exactly what I meant. Do you know who Amelia Earhart was?" T.J. asked.

"Sure." Lindsey earned straight A's with little effort. She knew about a lot of things. "Amelia Earhart was a famous pilot a long time ago."

Andrew's fair, freckled face turned red. "I thought she had something to do with a brand of luggage."

Ben laughed which made Lindsey start giggling as well.

Andrew frowned. "Mom has some old suitcases that say Amelia Hairtart on them."

Now Lindsey and Ben howled. Even T.J. snickered. Lindsey was used to her brother's dyslexia—the way he switched letters around—but sometimes it got her going.

"I'm sorry, Andrew," she said between laughs. "You just come out with the funniest things!"

"Yeah, I'm sorry, too," Ben said.

"Sure, until the next time I say something weird," Andrew grumbled.

"T.J., what about Amelia Earhart?" Lindsey asked, changing the subject.

"I think about her a lot when I fly."

"Why?"

"She was a great pilot, but she battled airsickness every time she flew. It just makes me feel like I'm in good company."

"Wow!" Lindsey's eyes widened. "I never knew she got airsick. I thought she was a really strong person."

"Lindsey!" Andrew said in a scolding tone.

"What? What did I say?" She pointed to herself.

Her brother rolled his eyes. "Not all people who get airsick are weaklings, you know."

"Oh, T.J.!" she cried. "I didn't mean you were weak or anything."

"That's all right," he said and smiled. "Planes were awkwardly built years ago when Amelia flew. They weren't user friendly, as we might say today. Flying upset most people's stomachs. In fact, one of the first commercial airlines boasted that only 75 percent of its passengers had ever gotten airsick." T.J. paused, and Lindsey wondered if he was about to be ill. But then he went on. "In my opinion, Amelia Earhart was very brave to fly."

"Oh, absolutely!" Lindsey wanted to get back in T.J.'s good graces. She liked her teacher a lot.

"When did Amelia Earhart live?" Ben asked.

T.J. didn't respond. Instead, he got up quickly and headed for the bathroom.

A flight attendant blocked his path. "Sir, you can't leave your seat yet," she said.

"It can't be helped!" T.J. put his mouth against the airsick bag, and the woman stepped out of his way—quickly.

"Poor T.J.!" Lindsey watched as he fled toward the restroom.

"You didn't make him feel any better, you know," Andrew said.

"Well, I'm sorry! I didn't mean to be rude."

"All right already." Andrew turned to his cousin. "How are you doing, Ben?"

"Okay. I don't know if I'd rather get sick like T.J. or just scared the way I do."

Ever since his father had died in a car accident, Ben had been nervous about any kind of travel—especially the kind of time traveling that sometimes happened so unexpectedly when they were with T.J.

Lindsey went back to watching the ocean outside her window. She tried to remember more about Amelia Earhart. She could only recall that the aviator had disappeared during a flight. She didn't know when or how. Intrigued, she decided to ask T.J. about it when he returned.

A few minutes later, T.J. sank into his seat once more. His face looked even more pale.

"Are you okay?" Lindsey asked.

Andrew and Ben looked a bit worried as well.

"I'll be fine." T.J. yawned. "I'm just a little sleepy."

"Say, T.J., didn't Amelia Earhart disappear?" Lindsey asked, wanting to keep her teacher awake.

But their tutor had already fallen fast asleep. A victim of narcolepsy, T.J. could nod off any time, anywhere. It was a wonder he hadn't sleepwalked his way back from the restroom.

The sun streamed through the window, and Lindsey let it warm her face. Maybe it would help clear up her pimples. She'd read a magazine once that said something about the sun doing that. She turned to her brother. "Hey, Andrew, do you think…"

Suddenly Lindsey felt a strange sensation near her right elbow. It tingled where her arm touched Andrew's. The feeling spread up and down her arm and began filling her entire body.

"What's wrong?" Ben asked.

"I…I can't move."

Her cousin reached across the aisle to waken T.J., then, "Lindsey! I feel it, too!" Ben looked terrified.

"T.J. must have fallen asleep thinking about a mystery." Lindsey felt her strength drain. Right before she blacked out she heard Ben groan, "Oh, no! Not again!"

Chapter Two

Lindsey had come to expect certain things to happen when time traveling with T.J. Like awakening with a sore hand and finding herself in the clothes of whatever time and place they visited. Being known by those in the historic setting, as if she had always lived there. Having to pretend she was T.J.'s daughter because that's who everyone thought she was. And only getting home once they had solved a mystery.

Lindsey glanced around her. They seemed to be in a large warehouse of some kind. "I wonder where—"

Suddenly, out of nowhere, a huge German shepherd bounded after her and the boys, who stood beside her. The sleek animal barked savagely. Saliva dripped from its mouth as the charging dog bared its large, pointed teeth. Lindsey froze in terror.

"Hey, what's going on?" A man in a military uniform glowered at them. Then he ran after the dog, which was not on a leash. "Heel, Queenie! Heel!"

Andrew and Ben yanked at Lindsey's arms, pulling her out of the animal's path. She felt like a red cape in the hands of a matador.

"Ouch, guys! My arm!"

"More than that will hurt if that dog gets hold of you," Ben cried.

They burst through a nearby door and slammed it shut

right before the dog reached them. Queenie leaped and scratched at the flimsy aluminum door, trying to get at her prey. The soldier caught up with the animal.

"Stupid dog! Why didn't you heel?" he yelled.

Queenie pounced at the door again, and Lindsey was sure it would break open from the impact. She shrank against her brother and cousin.

"Heel!" the man shouted again, and the dog finally obeyed. He seized Queenie's collar and then led the dog away. "I'll be back!" he called over his shoulder.

"Th-that was scary!" She felt herself trembling.

Ben put his arm around her. "I'm sorry about your arm. Does it still hurt?"

"No. Thanks, Ben. It's okay now."

"Where are we?" Andrew asked.

No longer in immediate danger, Lindsey scanned their surroundings—a small office which smelled like oil and grease, much like a garage. A worn chair with a spring threatening to pop out reminded her of the waiting area in a gas station. Beyond the glass walls she saw a huge hollow space, the repair bays in a servicing area for cars, but much larger. And there were no cars. Then she saw the plane.

"Look at that!" Lindsey pointed out a silver aircraft unlike any she had ever seen before.

"That's really cool!" Andrew cried.

"It's so old-looking," Ben said.

"It must be pretty important. It's the only one in the place, and there's lots of room for more planes," Lindsey said. "I guess this must be the hangar of an airport."

"Yes, but where?" Ben asked.

"There's T.J.!" Andrew pointed to a small group of people. Two looked like mechanics, and the other handful were as well-dressed as T.J. They had just emerged from behind the elegant plane.

"I see him!" Lindsey said. "I wonder what he's doing, though. He's so dressed up."

Ben giggled. "I've never seen him in a suit before. It even has one of those pocket handkerchiefs."

"You look pretty cute yourselves," Lindsey said, giving her brother and cousin a once-over.

Ben and Andrew looked down at their fancy outfits and groaned. They liked jeans and T-shirts as a rule.

"Well, look at your dress, Lindsey," Ben said. "Those buttons are so big."

"And it's so droopy."

"What do you mean, Andrew?" Lindsey craned for a better look at herself.

"It sort of falls at the middle." He put his hands at his waist, then let them fall to explain what he meant.

"Oh, I see. It's called a drop waist." Lindsey frowned. "It's not very flattering. I feel huge." She looked into a cracked mirror on a wall near the door. "And I still have my braces." She sighed loudly. "Now, then, where could we be? Let's find out what we can before that soldier comes back."

"Maybe we should leave. Make a beeline for T.J. or something," Andrew said.

Suddenly the door opened and a different man entered the room.

"Well, hello, kids!" he said. "I wondered what happened to you. T.J. said you were here somewhere."

The man was almost six feet tall, distinguished-looking, and probably about fifty years old. He had gray hair mixed with a lot of brown. He looked wealthy, judging from the obvious quality and tailoring of his clothes.

The soldier returned then. "Do you know them?" he asked in a surprised tone.

"Of course. They're T.J. Wakesnoris's kids. Don't tell me Queenie attacked them." His face reddened in anger.

"I'm afraid so, G.P." Now it was the soldier's turn to look nervous.

"Was the beast on its leash?"

"No, sir, she wasn't."

"Well, make sure she is from now on. Queenie's here to keep intruders out, not tear our friends to pieces or scare them to death."

"Sorry, G.P. Sorry, kids!"

"Sure, that's okay," they all muttered half-heartedly.

Just who was this G.P. guy?

"Just stay put for a few minutes," G.P. said. "We'll come back for you, and then we can go on to the house. Mrs. DeCarrie has everything ready for you. You're probably tired from your trip."

The two men turned and walked out of the room.

"Who's Mrs. DeCarrie?" Ben asked.

"Or G.P. for that matter?"

"Does he know we time traveled?" Andrew's blue eyes widened.

"One question at a time!" Lindsey said. "He probably thinks we got here in the normal way, by plane, bus, or train. I don't know who he is, though. Let's try to put some pieces together." She began to pace the small office. "Our clothes remind me of being at Loch Ness, Scotland."

"How do you mean?" Andrew cocked his head.

"They seem to be from the same time period, the 1930s."

"But this isn't Loch Ness, is it?" Ben looked a bit panicky. "We're not stuck there, are we, like we'll keep going back there time after time? Remember that movie *Groundhog Day?* Every time this reporter woke up, it was February 2, and he was in Punxsutawney waiting for the groundhog to see its shadow."

"No, Ben, I don't think it's anything like that." The idea did make Lindsey feel somewhat uneasy, though. "Anyway, it's too warm to be Scotland. I'm sweating under this heavy dress." Lindsey wanted to reassure her cousin. "And look!" She directed their attention to a large American flag, which hung from a rafter in the hangar.

"We're in America, then," Andrew said. "I'm glad of that."

"But where in America?" Lindsey asked.

"Hey, there's a calendar!" Ben led them to a blotter on the desk. He pushed his glasses up on his nose as he studied the page in front of him. "April 1937."

"Three years later than our last adventure," Andrew said.

"At least by time travel standards." Lindsey became thoughtful. "Back home it's only been a few months since we solved the Loch Ness Monster mystery."

"Yeah, well, at least your friend Sarah Sleeth didn't come with us this time." Andrew grinned.

"I like Sarah!"

"Oh, she's a bundle of laughs," her brother teased.

Lindsey watched as T.J. and his companions walked slowly around the unmarked plane. They looked so serious, and she wondered whether something might be wrong.

She started thinking out loud again. "Let's see, 1937. Who was president then?"

"Franklin Roosevelt," Ben said.

"And there was a depression on," Lindsey added.

"Is that the same one they talked about at Loch Ness?" Andrew asked.

She nodded. "It went on for a really long time. All during the '30s, I think. It ended when World War II started. That was like 1941 or something."

"You sure know your history." Andrew shook his head. "But you know something, I don't mind learning it this way. From a book it stinks."

Lindsey laughed.

"Give me a book anytime," Ben said. "I'm always afraid we won't get back when we time travel with T.J."

"Oh, you of little faith!" Lindsey poked him, then she said, "I wonder what mystery this could be. What was T.J. thinking about right before he fell asleep?"

For each of their adventures, they had learned that when their teacher fell asleep while thinking hard about an unsolved mystery, they all went back to that place and time.

"Let's see, you were talking about that female pilot," Andrew said.

"Amelia Earhart!" Ben said.

"That's right, Ben!" Lindsey made a fist and hit her palm with it. "I was asking about her disappearance. I wanted to find out what happened to her."

Just then the door squeaked open, and Lindsey nearly jumped out of her skin.

"So sorry!" said the tall, lean woman standing in the doorway. Her short blond hair was tousled, and her smile revealed a gap between two front teeth. "I didn't mean to startle you so."

Lindsey gaped. She'd seen this woman before somewhere. The yellow jumpsuit and scarf tied nattily around her neck seemed so familiar. Could it be?

"I hear old Queenie gave you a start, too. That's no way to welcome our friends." Suddenly her clear blue eyes clouded, and her voice hardened. "Some people around here are going too far with all this." Then, just as quickly, she became cordial again. "Anyway, we'll be ready to leave in a few minutes. Your father's just completing his inspection of the plane. I'm so glad he could come. I don't know what I'd do without his advice. He sees things no one else does."

G.P. returned to the office then and gave the woman a sideways hug. "Hello, kids!" he said. "I see you've met Amelia Earhart."

Chapter Three

Amelia Earhart! To think that Lindsey Skillman was about to unravel the mystery of this famous woman's disappearance! It didn't get any better than that.

"We're just getting acquainted," the famous flyer told G.P., then turned back to Lindsey and the boys. "I haven't learned all your names yet."

Lindsey took charge. "I'm Lindsey Sk—uh, Wakesnoris." She had to constantly remind herself that she was T.J.'s daughter whenever they time traveled. She assumed that Ben was her brother, as in their other adventures. She introduced him and Andrew to Amelia Earhart.

"How nice to meet you," Amelia said. "I believe you know my husband, George Palmer Putnam, or G.P. as everyone calls him."

"Hello, Mr. Putnam." Lindsey reached out to shake his hand.

Andrew stared at Amelia. "If his last name is Putnam, why is yours Earhart?" he asked.

Lindsey rolled her eyes. Eager to please Miss Earhart, she quickly said, "Andrew, it's the name people know her by. A lot of women keep their names professionally." Her eyes bored into his.

"So, how old are all of you?" G.P. asked, changing the subject.

"I'm twelve," Ben said.

"I'm eleven," Andrew said proudly.

"And I'm thirteen." Lindsey was curious about Amelia's and G.P.'s ages, but she knew better than to ask—it wasn't polite. He looked much older than his wife. Amelia looked at least as old as Lindsey's parents, somewhere around forty, only the woman's face had a lot more lines than either Dr. or Mrs. Skillman's. Still, Lindsey thought she was beautiful, tall and thin and fashionable, even in a shapeless jump suit. Oh, to look like that, rather than like a dumpy kid! Lindsey had always been small, but over the last few months had started to fill out across rather than up. She felt awkward around this graceful woman. What a shame she couldn't at least have left her braces behind!

"It will be nice to have you stay with us," Amelia said. "I love having children around. G.P.'s two sons grew up so fast."

Lindsey's jaw dropped. "We're going to stay at your house?"

"Of course. Mrs. DeCarrie, our housekeeper, has everything ready. Let's go find T.J. and be off. I'm starving."

They joined T.J. near the plane. Queenie barked a few times, but she was tied up now. While the boys looked the plane over, Lindsey tried to get her teacher's attention.

"Yes, what is it, Lindsey?" he asked after two important-looking men finally quit talking to him.

"You've taken us back to Amelia Earhart's time," she whispered. Still, the excitement in her voice made the dog bark again.

"That's right."

"This is so exciting, T.J.!"

"Uh, better go back to calling me 'Dad' or 'Father.'"

"Oops, I forgot." Lindsey clapped her hand over her mouth. "Oh, thank you—uh—Dad. Amelia's the greatest! Isn't she beautiful?"

"I think someone has a crush," he said, smiling gently.

Lindsey frowned. "I thought crushes only applied to guys."

"Not always. Young girls often become charmed by accomplished older women. Amelia Earhart is, after all, very admirable."

Lindsey grinned shyly. "I guess I must have a crush on her, then. So, what are you supposed to be doing for her? Miss Earhart told us she didn't know what she'd do without you."

"Later, Lindsey."

"But—"

"There are too many people around."

Lindsey knew better than to argue with T.J. He meant no when he said it.

Moments later she found herself and the other Dreamers in the back of a 1930s limousine. She and the boys filled the farthest back seat, while T.J., Amelia, and G.P. sat in the seat opposite, facing them. A man in an army uniform drove. In fact, the place crawled with army personnel. Many military planes sat on the tarmac in readiness for their next flights. The warm April weather and the palm trees everywhere made Lindsey wonder if they might be in Hawaii, after all. Wouldn't that be wild?

Andrew corrected that idea quickly, however. He nudged Lindsey and pointed to a sign as the car passed through a gate guarded by a soldier.

"March Army Air Base," he said quietly.

Lindsey tilted her head for a better view. "Look, Ben," she said softly, pointing to the sign. He nodded. Just where was this air base, though? In what city or state? And what was Amelia Earhart doing at an army base?

This was too exciting! Another mystery!

G.P. did most of the talking during the trip that took a little over an hour. He had a high opinion of himself; he bragged a lot about his publishing business and also mentioned President and Mrs. Roosevelt's personal interest in Amelia's career—several times.

Amelia had been friendly with Lindsey and the boys at first, but now she simply sat quietly while her husband chattered. Lindsey kept listening and looking for clues as to their whereabouts. It was driving her crazy that she didn't know. Just when she thought she'd burst if she didn't find out, Andrew pointed to a huge billboard way up on a hill.

"Look!" he cried.

Lindsey bounced up and down in her seat. "It's the Hollywood sign!"

So that's where they were—Hollywood, California.

G.P. laughed. "Are you fond of movies?"

"Sure!" Andrew said.

"Who's your favorite star?"

"Uh, Kellie Martin, I guess."

Lindsey rolled her eyes and sighed softly. Kellie Martin wasn't alive in the 1930s. Her parents hadn't even been born then.

G.P. scratched his chin. "I can't say I've heard of her. How about you, Lindsey, whose name, I might add, reminds me of Lindbergh?"

"Who's that—" Ben began, but Lindsey pressed hard on his

foot with her own. Ben glared at her but kept quiet.

"Yes, it does sound like Lindbergh." Lindsey turned to T.J., appealing with her eyes for help.

"G.P. is quite fond of Colonel Lindbergh," he said, picking up the hint. "I am as well. I remember when he became the first man to fly across the Atlantic Ocean."

"I have to watch myself, though," G.P. said, winking at his wife. "I think there's a physical resemblance between my wife and Colonel Lindbergh. When I first started to publicize Amelia's flights, I called her 'Lady Lindy.'" He squeezed his wife's shoulder affectionately. "She quickly put a stop to that. My wife's accomplishments stand on their own."

Lindsey hoped that G.P. had forgotten about movie stars. He hadn't.

"So, Lindsey, who's your favorite actor?"

She racked her brain. What could she possibly know about movie stars from the 1930s?

"I don't let the children see many movies," T.J. said, rescuing her. "But when they do, Lindsey enjoys Shirley Temple."

"Yes, I guess she would," G.P. said.

"And the boys like Gary Cooper."

"A promising young actor."

Lindsey and the boys exchanged glances. "Whoever they are!" their looks said.

They finally pulled up in front of a beautiful, two-story home near a golf course. As they climbed out of the car, G.P. explained that they hadn't lived there very long.

"Amelia loves California. So does her mother. We've just put on an addition so that she can live with us more comfortably. It was pretty cramped with the three of us before."

Lindsey inhaled deeply. The pleasant fragrances of riotous flower borders and orange trees mingled delightfully. In the distance a gardener was cutting the grass with an ancient-looking power mower.

"This is beautiful, Miss Earhart!"

Amelia smiled. "G.P. and I love gardening."

"Although we employ a gardener because of Amelia's traveling," G.P. added, "the two of us dig in when we're at home."

"Come," Amelia said, "I'll introduce you to our housekeeper. She'll get you settled."

Once inside, Lindsey noticed that like its owner, the home was uncluttered and attractive. The neutral-colored furniture in the living room looked expensive. With her keen sense of smell, she sniffed a combination of lemons and baking bread. Her stomach began to rumble.

"Hello, Amelia," a crisp-looking woman with steel gray hair greeted them. "I'm ready for your guests."

Another younger woman burst into the room. "Mother, I must see Amelia. That Mr. Baruch is driving me crazy."

"In a minute, Margot," Amelia said. "First let me introduce our guests. This is T.J. Wakesnoris, who is advising me about the flight. These are his children, Lindsey, Ben, and Andrew. And this is Mrs. DeCarrie, our housekeeper. Her daughter, Margot, is my personal secretary."

Except for a slight resemblance in the face, the two women couldn't have looked more different. Margot had curly black hair, a willowy body, and romantic-looking clothes. Her much shorter mother was built like a Range Rover. She looked every inch the efficient housekeeper, from her sensible shoes to her stiff apron and head cap.

"Now, I'm all yours, Margot. T.J., please come with me. I'll need your advice about Fred Noonan."

Who was he? Lindsey wondered.

The two women, T.J., and G.P. went into a den and closed the door, while Mrs. DeCarrie took Lindsey and the boys upstairs.

T.J. had the first bedroom at the top of the stairs, and Lindsey's was to the left, a sunny yellow room with a wall of windows. The boys' bedroom was on the other side of T.J.'s.

"There's your private bathroom." Mrs. DeCarrie pointed to a door next to Lindsey's room. "Please wash up and come down to dinner in a half hour." She paused, folding her bare arms over her chest. "Does that give you enough time, Lindsey?"

"I guess so," Lindsey said doubtfully. She felt a bit nervous around this woman. She wasn't used to servants. "What should I wear to dinner?"

Mrs. DeCarrie's narrow brown eyes sized her up. "We are having a rather formal meal tonight. Government big shots." She sniffed her disapproval. "Didn't anyone bring your luggage in, young lady?"

"I, uh, don't think so." In her first adventure to the Lost Colony, she hadn't had luggage either. Was that going to happen here as well? Or would it be like Scotland, where she and the Dreamers had plenty of clothes?

The housekeeper shook her head. "I could let you borrow something of Miss Earhart's."

Wow! To wear something of Amelia Earhart's! But her heart sank with Mrs. DeCarrie's next comment. "She's a lot taller and thinner than you, though. I'll fix something up, but we'll have

to hurry. We'll go shopping tomorrow." She practically flew
toward the stairs. "I suppose your poor father's got his hands
full enough with three children and no wife. Wash up, Lindsey,
and I'll dig something out of Miss Amelia's closet for you."

At seven o'clock sharp Lindsey entered the formal dining room,
and was it ever formal! Heavy, English-printed chintz curtains
and an impressive Queen Anne table dominated the room. A
gorgeous floral centerpiece graced the crystal and china-laden
table. Everyone was dressed up—the Putnams, an older
woman who must be Amelia's mother, and a man Lindsey had
seen with T.J. at the hangar where the plane was kept. Ben and
Andrew had combed their hair back to freshen up, but they
were wearing the same outfits as before. T.J. had apparently
borrowed one of G.P.'s dressier suits.

"Well, look at you, Lindsey!" G.P. took her by the hands
and swung her around for everyone to see. "You look even
nicer in that dress than my wife does."

"You do look sweet, Lindsey," Amelia said. She wore a
smart silk dress in navy that sported some type of aviation pin
at the throat.

Lindsey had to suck in her stomach so the waist in her
ivory-colored dress didn't split. Mrs. DeCarrie was in a hurry,
and had quickly let out the hips and tacked up the hemline
with some kind of tape. Lindsey would have to be careful not
to eat too much.

"Amelia Two," G.P. said as he surveyed Lindsey. He looked
enormously pleased with himself for coming up with the nickname. "That's what I'll call you—Amelia, Two."

Lindsey burned with embarrassment as he introduced her and the boys to Bernard Baruch and Mrs. Amy Earhart. She hoped she didn't get confused with "Miss Earhart" and "Mrs. Earhart." How did the poor mailman keep everyone in this household straight?

During the meal, Lindsey carefully watched Amelia. The woman talked little, but Lindsey studied her every move. She was amazed to see the aviator frequently resting her elbows on the table. That was a no-no in the Skillman home. Amelia's mother kept reminding her to keep her hands in her lap, but Amelia couldn't seem to help herself. Other than that, like Amelia, Mrs. Earhart didn't say much. When Mr. Baruch asked how she liked living with her daughter, the older woman acted like she hadn't heard him.

"Mother, Mr. Baruch wants to know how you like it here." Amelia repeated the question in a loud, slow voice. Apparently her mother was hard of hearing.

"Oh, just fine," Mrs. Earhart said, sipping her soup.

Over pot roast and tiny red potatoes, Lindsey learned that Mr. Baruch served as a special advisor to President Roosevelt. He was tall and broad with a massive head of white hair. His pink cheeks seemed out of place. And he treated Mrs. DeCarrie rather rudely, Lindsey thought. At one point during the meal he lifted his plate to her, saying, "I'd like more roast, but don't put gravy on it this time. I asked you not to once before."

"Of course, sir," the housekeeper muttered and hurried to the kitchen.

Although she enjoyed the wonderful food and general conversation, Lindsey wanted to get T.J. alone. She wanted to know what Amelia was up to. Obviously she was planning a flight. But where was she going and why?

When it was time for dessert, Mrs. DeCarrie brought out plates of steaming apple cobbler. She placed one in front of Amelia Earhart, and Lindsey couldn't believe her eyes when G.P. abruptly pushed it away. Both the housekeeper and Amelia glared at him.

"You remember our bargain, Amelia?" G.P. said. "No dessert until you autograph twenty-five photos."

"But, G.P., we have company."

"Stop whimpering, Amelia. A deal's a deal."

Lindsey watched in amazement as Amelia Earhart took the photos from her husband and dutifully signed them. Only then did she get her cobbler. Andrew and Lindsey exchanged glances.

The only other problem they faced at the table was when T.J. started falling asleep over his coffee. Andrew kicked him under the table, which woke him up every time.

After dinner, Lindsey went up to T.J., hoping to pull him away from Bernard Baruch and G.P. Unfortunately, they had other plans.

"Come to the den, T.J.," Baruch said, steering the redhead away from his "children." "We have a lot to discuss."

Lindsey must have looked as disappointed as she felt. Before he walked away, T.J. called over his shoulder, "I'll come in later to say good night."

Chapter Four

Lindsey paced like a caged tiger. How could anyone expect her to go to bed at eight-thirty? Was she supposed to stay in her room, or was she free to roam the house? Maybe a magazine would get her mind off the mystery until T.J. finished downstairs. She had seen a copy of *Redbook* in the bathroom. She restlessly leafed through the articles on home, health, and beauty, but none of them held her attention.

A half hour later she gave up. It was no use. She had to know what was going on in the den. T.J. might not finish with those men and Amelia until really late. If so, he would probably decide not to awaken her and the boys. As if she could sleep without knowing what was going on!

Maybe the boys would go downstairs with her. That way at least she wouldn't be alone if she got into trouble for leaving her room. There had to be a way to find out what was going on in the den.

She looked into the hallway to make sure the coast was clear, then tip-toed out of her room. At that moment a gust of wind blew through the bedroom, and the door slammed behind her with a jarring smack. She nearly jumped out of her skin.

"What was that?" Mrs. DeCarrie called sharply from the bottom of the stairs.

"Uh, my door slammed—from the wind," Lindsey

returned. "Sorry about the noise."

"As long as you're all right." The housekeeper paused. "Do you need anything, Lindsey?"

Yeah, more information, she said to herself. Out loud she said, "No, thank you."

After Mrs. DeCarrie left, Lindsey stepped across the hall to the boys' room and knocked. No one answered. That was strange. Surely they wouldn't be asleep at nine o'clock. She waited a few moments to make sure Mrs. DeCarrie was really gone. Then she slipped downstairs and wandered toward the living room, which was situated next to the den. It would be the best place to listen in on Amelia's gathering.

Lindsey's heart quickened as she turned the knob to the French doors. When she opened the door she was surprised to find Andrew and Ben sitting on the couch reading books. Andrew never read anything he didn't have to.

"Oh, it's you," Ben whispered, letting out a deep breath. "I thought we were going to get caught."

"Caught?" Lindsey moved closer to see the title of her brother's book. "*The Decline of the Hapsburg Empire*?" He couldn't possibly be really reading that. "What are you doing?"

Andrew put the book on the coffee table. "Mrs. DeCarrie thinks we're in here reading," he said in a low tone. "You're not the only one who wants to know what's going on."

Her ears perked up. "You mean you can hear what they're saying?"

Ben nodded as laid his book down, too. "Not every word, but enough to make it interesting."

Lindsey scooted next to them on the couch. "So, what's up?"

"Lots, let me tell you."

"Well, tell me, Ben," she said impatiently.

"And miss what they're saying right now?" Ben asked.

"Just tell me enough to bring me up to date."

Ben explained that Amelia was getting ready to fly around the world, and the U.S. government was paying for it. "They have to keep it secret, though. Lots of people are out of work and would be mad if they knew."

"I guess so." Lindsey became thoughtful. "Imagine trying to go around the world in a 1930s plane!" She shuddered. "I thought Amelia and G.P. were rich. Just look at this house." She gestured to the custom-made curtains and original paintings.

Ben shook his head. "They used a lot of their savings when she made the first attempt in March."

"I'm confused," Lindsey said. "She tried this before?"

Andrew nodded. "But she wrecked the plane on the runway."

"And it would've cost a fortune to fix it, so the government is fixing it for her," Ben said.

"But why?" Lindsey asked.

Andrew leaned closer to his sister. "There are a lot of people in this meeting, and Baruch and this other guy, Miller, want her to—"

Someone was at the door. Quickly the boys grabbed their books and pretended to read. Lindsey looked over her brother's shoulder and tried to seem interested in his book.

"Do you need anything?" Mrs. DeCarrie asked.

"No, thanks," they answered.

The housekeeper frowned. "You'd better go on up to bed now."

Lindsey led the way, disappointed to be leaving just as things were getting interesting.

"Good night, Mrs. DeCarrie," she said.

"Good night, dear. Good night, boys."

"Good night, Mrs. DeCarrie," Andrew and Ben said together.

Lindsey giggled as they approached the stairs. "We sounded like the Waltons with all those good nights!"

"What now?" Andrew asked.

Suddenly the door to the den opened, and people spilled out of the room, talking loudly.

"This has been productive, gentlemen," G.P.'s voice rose above the others'. "I think we have a win-win situation."

"Yes, I believe we do," one of the government men said.

As the adults drew closer, Lindsey and the boys scrambled upstairs.

"Let's go to T.J.'s room and wait for him," Lindsey suggested.

"Good idea," Ben agreed.

Moments later their teacher opened his door—and gasped. "You startled me. I didn't expect anyone to be in here."

Lindsey cut to the chase. "What's going on?"

"Why is Amelia going around the world?"

"Why is the government paying for it?"

"What's with the Japanese?"

"Slow down!" T.J. laughed. "How do you know all this?" He sank wearily into a rocking chair. There were dark circles under his eyes.

She pointed to the boys. "They were spying from the living room."

"Thanks, Lindsey," Andrew said.

T.J. shook his head. "I should've guessed it. I'll bet your

heads are swimming with what little you know."

"They are," Lindsey said. "We can't put all the pieces together either."

"Let's start at the beginning, then." T.J. removed his necktie and ran a hand through his reddish blond hair.

"Okay," Andrew said. "Just who is Amelia Earhart, besides a pilot and luggage?"

A clock ticked loudly in the background, and Lindsey heard footsteps below them on the first floor.

"Amelia is the most famous female aviator ever," T.J. said.

"How did she get started?" Lindsey asked.

"After World War I she went to California to recover from an illness. A friend took her to an air show, and she fell in love with planes. She took flying lessons and got a license."

"When did she get famous?" asked Ben.

"Well, a group of flyers and navigators had talked about being the first to cross the Atlantic with a woman. This was in 1928, the year after Charles Lindbergh became the first person to do so." T.J. yawned and, one by one, the others followed. "What a day!" he said. "Anyway, G.P. was publicizing the flight—this was before they were married—and he picked Amelia Earhart to be the woman. They got married a few years later. Anyway, Amelia made history when she became the first woman to fly the Atlantic Ocean. But she was still only a passenger—she wanted to set her own aviation records."

"What did she do?" asked Andrew.

"She was the first woman to cross the Atlantic alone. She also soloed from Hawaii to California. Then, on top of that, she set a number of speed records flying across the United States and back."

Lindsey considered all this. "So we're in 1937 now, right?"

T.J. nodded. "A month ago Amelia set out to make an around-the-world flight at the equator. No one else had done that yet. She started in California and got as far as Hawaii."

"She crashed the plane trying to take off," Ben added. "It was loaded down with fuel, and the runway wasn't in good condition."

T.J.'s eyes widened. "You did hear a lot."

"Was anyone hurt?" Lindsey asked.

"No, thank God. Amelia's getting ready to give it another try now." T.J. stared into space. When he began dozing off, Lindsey nudged him, and he jerked awake. "Huh? What?"

"You were telling us about Amelia trying to make the around-the-world flight again." Lindsey paused. "You know, T.J., that plane we saw today is in great shape for having been in an accident."

"It certainly is."

"And you're supposed to be one of her trusted advisors, right?" Lindsey asked.

"Amelia wants me to operate the radio in San Francisco. I'll be in fairly close touch with her during the flight."

"How cool!" Lindsey was beside herself. "How do you know about radios, and what will you do exactly?"

"My dad is an avid ham-radio operator, so I grew up with that," T.J. said. "I also was a radio DJ in college. I'm no expert by our time's standards, but according to 1937 technology I am. As for what I'll be doing, I'll give Amelia weather reports, find out if the plane needs repairs or parts, and then make sure she has them at her next stop."

"Will you do it by yourself?"

"No. There are other radio operators, but G.P. and I will be the most closely connected."

"T.J., I know that Amelia Earhart disappeared during one of her flights," Lindsey said. "Is this the one?"

"Yes." He nodded soberly.

"She disappeared?" asked Ben. "How?"

"No one knows exactly. During the flight, she went down somewhere in the Pacific."

"Was she alone?" Lindsey asked.

"She was with her navigator, a guy named Fred Noonan. We haven't met him yet."

"I've wondered who he was since I first heard his name," Lindsey said. "So then, we'll find out what happened to her, right?"

"It looks that way," T.J. said. "I think God has given us another opportunity to solve one of history's great mysteries."

"This is so cool!" Andrew exclaimed.

"Speaking of God," Ben said. "Are the Earharts—or rather, Putnams—Christians?"

"What a question!" Lindsey gave her hair a toss. "Of course Amelia Earhart was a Christian."

"How do you know?" Ben asked.

"Well, first of all, we said grace before we ate tonight." She faltered. That sounded pretty lame. "Of course, maybe G.P. isn't. He's pretty hard on her. I don't think the way he made her sign those pictures would please the Lord."

"Lindsey, Amelia Earhart is kind, and she's brave," T.J. said. "But that doesn't automatically mean she's a believer. The question is whether or not she has a personal relationship with Christ. We'll just have to see how that plays out." T.J. spoke in a gentle yet firm manner.

"She must be," Lindsey persisted. "She's the neatest person I've ever met. Really neat people know God."

"I hope she's a believer, too," T.J. said, nodding, "but if she's not, we might be able to influence her."

Andrew frowned. "I thought we couldn't change the way mysteries turn out. We only find out what happened."

"That's right," T.J. said.

"So, if Amelia's not a Christian, how can we change that?"

"That's not exactly the same as changing the course of history. When it comes to God and the human heart, nothing is impossible."

A few moments passed, and then Lindsey asked, "T.J., is the government involved because of Miss Earhart's friendship with President and Mrs. Roosevelt?"

"No." Lowering his voice even further, T.J. said, "There's a great deal more to it than that. The public has no idea what's really going on here."

Chapter Five

Lindsey leaned forward to catch every word. Amelia Earhart, America's sweetheart, had become a spy.

T.J. explained that the Japanese were building an empire in the Pacific by seizing control of its islands. It didn't matter to whom they belonged. President Roosevelt feared that American interests in the Pacific might be threatened. And if Japan got especially strong, it might even attack the United States mainland. But the American people were in an anti-war mood. So was Congress, and FDR's hands were tied.

"The government has made a secret deal with Amelia," T.J. said. "It will pay for her second attempt to fly around the world. In return she'll take pictures of Japanese military activity in the Pacific region. This is a secret because Congress and the public don't care what other countries do. They want America to keep to itself."

"Why?" Lindsey asked.

"The United States was trying to pull out of the depression. They also didn't want to get into another war because World War I had been so awful."

"I thought we were like the world's policemen or something," Ben said, pushing up his glasses.

"Not until after the Second World War in the 1940s."

"There were an awful lot of wars," Andrew said.

"Yes, and Americans wanted to stay out of them."

Lindsey wanted to get everything straight. "So Amelia's going to spy on the Japanese so she can make her record-breaking flight and help her country?"

T.J. nodded. "By accomplishing this mission, she just might be able to keep us out of a war. Amelia will also test some new radio equipment for possible military use."

Lindsey felt her eyes misting. "Amelia Earhart put her life on the line for her country. What a hero!"

"Yes, she's a hero, Lindsey."

They heard footsteps on the landing and fell silent. When whoever it was had passed, Lindsey spoke first—quietly.

"So the public doesn't have a clue what's going on here?"

"No." T.J. shook his head.

"Isn't anyone even asking? I mean, some of these things are pretty suspicious, like Amelia's plane being at a military base."

"And how the president's men are hanging around her," Andrew added.

"And look how quickly she fixed her plane," Ben said, "even though the Putnams don't have a lot of money."

T.J. rocked thoughtfully in his chair. "America was very different in the 1930s. People trusted the government to do the right things. They even trusted the press."

"That's incredible!" Andrew said.

"I guess we've solved the mystery, then," Ben said. "Since we know why Amelia Earhart went on this flight, we can go home, right?"

"We do know that part, but we haven't solved the most baffling thing of all," T.J. said. "You see, Amelia never made it around the world. When she got to the place where she was supposed to be spying, she vanished."

"Didn't anyone ever hear from her again?" Lindsey asked.

"Not according to the story."

"Do you believe it?"

"Not anymore, Lindsey. Not after what I learned tonight. This mystery is far from solved."

The next morning Mrs. DeCarrie took Lindsey and the boys shopping for new clothes. It was obvious that the housekeeper took this job very seriously, unlike Lindsey's mother, who "got it over with." You went in, you got what you needed, you left. For Mrs. DeCarrie, however, shopping was a grand event. She dragged the Dreamers into one fashionable store after another, barely listening to the boys' protests about her choices. Mrs. DeCarrie knew what boys who stayed with Amelia Earhart should look like.

Lindsey had to laugh at her suddenly formal brother and cousin. Their suits, sport coats, shirts, and ties were so unlike what they usually wore—jeans, T-shirts, athletic shoes. Even their so-called play clothes looked fancy—all tweeds, twills, belts, and leather shoes.

"This is the pits," Andrew complained loudly when Mrs. DeCarrie went off to put their names in for lunch at a fashionable restaurant. In the background a pianist in a tux played Vivaldi.

"You don't like your new clothes, do you?" Lindsey asked, holding several bags full of outfits. Most of them were dressier than she liked, too, but Mrs. DeCarrie had permitted her to get a few Amelia Earhart-type outfits as well. Lindsey wondered who was paying for all these things.

"I can hardly breathe under these stiff collars." Ben ran an index finger along the inside of one.

"And I can hardly breathe in all this smoke," Lindsey said, coughing.

"And stinky perfume," her brother added.

Lindsey's eyes ran the length of the expensively furnished restaurant. The customers, mostly women, wore fancy hats, high heels, and dripped with jewelry. Not everyone was out of work in the 1930s, at least not in Hollywood.

"You made out all right, Lindsey," Ben said in an obvious effort to be positive.

"I think so." She beamed happily.

"Amelia Two."

"Well, I like the clothes she wears. She always looks so sharp."

"And you want to be just like her, right?" Andrew said.

Lindsey hesitated. "Well, not exactly."

"I know you. You get on these kicks with people, and then you wear your hair like them."

Lindsey patted her shoulder-length hair. She had purposely tried that morning to make it look carefree, like Amelia's. Instead it simply looked uncombed.

"Then you intimidate their clothes," Andrew went on.

"Imitate," she corrected him, putting her hands on her hips. "And when have I done that?"

Ben giggled. "I hate to remind you, Lindsey, but last year you got on that kick with the skater, remember? She wore lots of rings, so you did, too."

Lindsey waved a hand. "This isn't the same thing. Amelia Earhart is a true hero. I want to be just like her someday."

"Seems you've already started," Andrew said, elbowing Ben, and then they snickered.

"Amelia Two," they said in unison.

Lindsey stuck her chin up. "She's my mentor."

Now Andrew reared back and howled. At that moment Mrs. DeCarrie returned. "Really, Andrew!" she said, which shut him up immediately. "Come, children. They have a place for us."

"Already!" Lindsey said in surprise. "There are at least ten people ahead of us."

"When you're part of Amelia Earhart's household, you get special treatment," the housekeeper said proudly.

Lindsey enjoyed the fancy luncheon, although she wished Mrs. DeCarrie hadn't ordered escargots—snails—for an appetizer. They were chewy and disgusting, like eating a dirty eraser. The French onion soup was tastier, and the main course, Cornish game hen, was delicious. Once Lindsey put her elbows on the table, like Amelia had done the night before.

"That's improper for a young lady," Mrs. DeCarrie corrected her.

Lindsey removed her elbows from the table. "Amelia did it last night."

"And you may do it, too—once you've flown the Atlantic."

Just as the waitress served vanilla ice cream with raspberry sauce, Mrs. DeCarrie glanced toward the door and gasped. "There's Shirley Temple," she cried.

There was no mistaking the mop of curly hair, Shirley Temple's trademark. The maitre d' was practically falling all over the girl and the two women with her. Whenever Miss Temple smiled, her dimples deepened. She was so cute.

Suddenly a pang of jealousy shot through Lindsey. She felt awkward, like a three-legged cow. Shirley Temple was just a movie star, though. She probably wasn't smart like Amelia Earhart. Who wanted to be pretty and pert anyway? Miss Earhart was attractive—and smart to boot. And with her new clothes, Lindsey could start dressing just like her. Now if only she had Miss Earhart's slim body....

After lunch their driver, the soldier who had escorted them the day before, took a route through Beverly Hills to the Putnam residence. At one point Lindsey noticed a beautiful stone church.

"The Earharts, uh, I mean, Putnams, go to church, don't they?" she asked Mrs. DeCarrie.

"They were there for Easter."

"Oh! That's nice."

"Is it?" Mrs. DeCarrie frowned at Lindsey.

"Well, yes. I'm glad Amelia believes in God."

"She ought to. He's pulled her out of enough scrapes in those flying machines of hers."

"See," she mouthed to Andrew and Ben.

"Lindsey," Ben said softly, "you know that's not what makes someone a Christian."

"Mrs. DeCarrie, does Miss Earhart go to church any other time?" Lindsey wanted to prove that her hero was a believer, after all.

"Yes, at Christmas, or when there's a wedding or funeral."

"Oh," Lindsey said, disappointed. Oh, well. At least Amelia Earhart believed in God. That was a start.

When they arrived at the Putnams' house, Mrs. DeCarrie followed the Dreamers upstairs, where she helped the boys put their things away in their room. "I'll be with you shortly," she told Lindsey. "I need to gather extra hangers for your things."

While she waited, Lindsey sat at her white wicker vanity and tried again to arrange her hair like Amelia's. Now that she had the clothes, she needed the hairstyle. But the length made it difficult for her to get that tossed look. She finally gathered her hair into a loose ponytail, letting a few strands fall carelessly around her face.

Lindsey then dug into the bags of clothes and, ignoring the pretty skirts and dresses, found one of three new scarves. She climbed out of her new outfit, one Mrs. DeCarrie had assured her Amelia Earhart would like, and put on a pair of baggy trousers and a loose-fitting blouse. As a finishing touch, she tied the scarf around her throat, just the way Amelia wore hers.

"You do beat all!" Mrs. DeCarrie said from the doorway.

"W-what do you mean?" Lindsey asked, startled.

"With your hair like that and those clothes, you could be mistaken for Amelia's daughter."

Lindsey felt like she'd been handed the moon. "Do you really think so?"

"Yes, I do." Mrs. DeCarrie clucked her tongue. "Still and for all that I don't generally approve of girls wearing pants. The next thing you know, men will be wearing dresses!"

"Mrs. DeCarrie, Amelia doesn't have a daughter, does she?"

"Goodness, no! When would she have time?"

"Do you think she'll mind that I look like her?"

"I doubt it." Mrs. DeCarrie started hanging things up in the closet. "Not with the weight of the world on her shoulders."

Lindsey was immediately curious. "What do you mean?"

The housekeeper didn't respond right away. Instead, she hung up a blouse, buttoning every button with irritating slowness. Lindsey was beside herself by the time Mrs. DeCarrie finally replied.

"Amelia hasn't been herself lately, and it has me concerned."

She acted like she wanted to say more. Lindsey would have to pull it out, little by little.

"How hasn't she been herself?"

"For one thing, during the last month she hasn't done much for publicity. That's unheard of around here."

Lindsey remembered the night before at dinner when G.P. had required Amelia to autograph pictures before she could eat her dessert. She mentioned the incident, then asked, "Wasn't that publicity?"

"Things were a little more normal in that respect last night. I think some photographer is supposed to do more pre-flight pictures in a day or so."

"But before this, Amelia hasn't done much publicity?"

Mrs. DeCarrie nodded. "Since the crash in March, she hasn't given any interviews. Also, her public appearances have been few and far between." She began removing sales tags from the clothes.

"Maybe the crash really upset her."

"Maybe." Mrs. DeCarrie sounded unconvinced, however. "She just mopes around here when she's home. She used to tell me everything, but not anymore. Amelia hardly speaks to anyone anymore." Mrs. DeCarrie vigorously snapped a tag off a scarf.

"There sure are a lot of people from the government around."

"That's another thing." The housekeeper waved a pair of scissors at Lindsey. Outside the open window a car door slammed. Mrs. DeCarrie looked to see if she was needed. "It's just G.P.," she said, sitting down on the side of the bed. "That Baruch person and that William Miller are here a good deal. Mr. Baruch has taken to sleeping here most of the time. They eat a good deal, too. Afterwards they go to the den with Amelia and speak in low tones for hours."

"Why do they come here so often?" Although Lindsey already knew, she wanted to find out just how informed Mrs. DeCarrie was.

"I'm not sure. They act like they own the place, though. It's 'Mrs. DeCarrie this,' and 'Mrs. DeCarrie that.'"

"Mr. Baruch wasn't very polite at dinner last night," Lindsey said, remembering his remark about the gravy.

"He never is. And another thing." She seemed to be on a roll. "The nicest man, Amelia's radio operator, hasn't been here since the March crash. I liked Walter so much." She spoke as if the man were dead.

"Walter?"

"Walter McMenamy."

"What happened to him?"

Mrs. DeCarrie shrugged. "Who knows? I guess Misters Baruch and Miller don't want him around. I can't imagine why, though. Walter is so trustworthy, so loyal to Amelia. Now everything's being done by the government, right down to keeping the plane at March Army Air Base." She fell silent, running her hand over the comforter's floral pattern. "There's another thing, although I don't know why I'm telling all of this to a young girl."

Lindsey hoped she wouldn't stop now. "People say I'm easy to talk to," she said, trying to reassure her.

"And so you are." She patted Lindsey's hand, then continued. "My daughter used to go fairly crazy trying to stay on top of all the bills that would roll in here."

"Bills?"

"For things like fuel and fixtures, radio equipment, and canvas. Whatever it takes to keep and maintain a plane. The Putnams had an awful time paying for all those things before." She glanced around furtively, as if someone could be listening, then lowered her voice. "Since those government men came, Margot hasn't received a single bill for the Electra's expenses."

"Is that the plane?"

Mrs. DeCarrie nodded.

It seemed obvious that no one had told Mrs. DeCarrie what was happening. Maybe that's why Amelia Earhart was keeping her distance from the housekeeper.

"What do you think those men are up to?" Lindsey asked.

Mrs. DeCarrie's face reddened, and her eyes flashed. "No good, that's what. Absolutely no good will come of whatever's going on here."

Chapter Six

"Too bad the boys are sleeping in and missing this breakfast." Lindsey wiped rich maple syrup from the corner of her mouth with a linen napkin.

"Andrew would probably just put ketchup on it, anyway," T.J. said, grinning.

She laughed merrily at T.J.'s remark. He was sure in a good mood today. "You must've slept well," she said.

"I did at that."

"So, where's everyone else?"

G.P. wasn't around. Nor was the ever-present Bernard Baruch or Amelia's mother.

"Maybe they're still sleeping."

"And maybe they're not," a female voice spoke from the doorway.

"Good morning," Lindsey and T.J. greeted Amelia Earhart.

"It is, too." Dressed in a pair of slacks suitable for horseback riding, and a plain silk blouse and scarf, Amelia looked like a schoolgirl. Lindsey couldn't help herself; she gaped in open adoration.

"Is it just the three of us?" Her eyes darted about the room.

"As far as I know," T.J. said.

"Where's G.P.?" Lindsey asked.

"He went golfing." A mischievous look came into Amelia's

eyes. "How would the two of you like to go with me on an adventure?"

Lindsey thought she might fly on her own strength, she was so excited. "Would I ever!"

"Adventure seems to be our middle name." T.J. winked at Lindsey.

"Let's go before anyone can stop us." Amelia giggled and clapped her hands.

"Where are we going?" Lindsey asked.

"Have you ever flown before?"

Had she flown before in the context of 1937? Amelia must have thought the Dreamers got to California in something other than a plane or she wouldn't have asked. Lindsey prayed quickly for guidance.

"I've always loved the idea of flying," she said. "Are you offering to take us?" This was beyond Lindsey's wildest imaginings.

"I sure am!" Amelia said. "Do you have any objections, T.J.? Some people think it's dangerous."

"None whatsoever," he answered graciously. He gave Lindsey a discreet thumbs up and formed the words "Nice job" with his lips.

"Then let's go!"

Lindsey and T.J. jumped up from their seats just as Mrs. DeCarrie entered the kitchen. "What in the world!" she exclaimed.

Amelia held a finger to her lips. "Not a word. We're adventure-bound."

The housekeeper's face broke into a grin. "Not a word. Just for my own peace of mind, though, where are you going, Amelia?"

"Flying. I'll borrow one of Paul's planes."

Lindsey wondered who Paul was as she followed Amelia and T.J. to the back door. She nearly crashed into the aviatrix, as women pilots were known then, when Amelia stopped for a leather jacket. She flung it over her right shoulder, then gazed keenly at Lindsey's outfit. Did she disapprove of her copying Amelia's style? Lindsey felt her hands go clammy.

"If you're going to imitate me, young lady, you'd better learn to tie that scarf properly," she said after a few heart-stopping moments. She reached down to retie it, and Lindsey's heart started beating normally again.

"I...I hope you don't mind," she said.

"Mind what? That you want to dress like me? Amelia Two and all that?"

"Well, yes." Lindsey was embarrassed that T.J. could hear this very private conversation.

"Lindsey, dear, it's normal to copy someone else while you're finding your own special style. I did when I was growing up."

"You did?"

T.J. turned to ask Mrs. DeCarrie what kind of coffee she used.

"Sure," Amelia said. "And someday in the not-too-distant future, you'll wake up and find a Lindsey Wakesnoris way that's just right for you. In the meantime, I'm flattered ten times over that a special girl like you has chosen to imitate me. I mean, you could've chosen Shirley Temple. I think most young girls would rather imitate her than an old person like me!"

Lindsey laughed. "You're not old. By the way, did Mrs. DeCarrie tell you we saw her at a restaurant yesterday?"

"No, but I'm not surprised. She's an adorable girl, isn't she?"

"Maybe that's why I don't want to look like her."

Amelia looked confused. "Because she's a little younger than you?"

"That, too. But it's mainly because she's so cute. I could never hope to look like that."

Amelia took Lindsey's hands in her own. They were rough, like her wind-blown, sun-exposed face. "You don't have to look like her. Besides, you are quite attractive yourself, Lindsey. I think you must be feeling awkward at your age, though. It's natural that you would. All girls do."

"Not Shirley Temple."

"Even Shirley Temple. You know, dear girl, beauty really is skin deep."

"I've heard that."

"Believe it!" She tugged playfully at Lindsey's scarf. "Enough said!" Amelia straightened up. She reached into the closet for an extra leather jacket, which she tossed at Lindsey, who nearly dropped it. "You may borrow this even though it'll be a bit bulky. It gets windy up there." She pointed to the sky. "T.J., do you have a jacket?"

"I'm not sure if I do," he said, turning back to them.

"Never mind. Take this." She handed him a tweed week-end jacket as they moved out the door. "You and G.P. are about the same size."

"Will that army guy drive us?" Lindsey asked. She felt all warm and glowy inside.

"Not today. We're taking my yellow monster."

Amelia led them to a three-car garage where she lifted one

of the doors, revealing a sleek yellow convertible with white-wall tires as dazzling as the sun on snow.

"It's a beauty!" Lindsey exclaimed, gawking.

"That's just what I was about to say." T.J. loved cars.

"Glad you like it." Amelia opened the driver's door as T.J. and Lindsey went around to the other side. T.J. sat in the back, and Lindsey climbed into the front beside Amelia.

"What kind of car is it?" Lindsey asked.

"A Cord Phaeton."

She'd never heard of such an exotic sounding car. "It sure is pretty."

"Thanks! I like it well enough."

Amelia swung the convertible out of the garage and turned onto Valley Spring Road. Lindsey held her blowing hair in place, but wisps of it still lashed at her face. At least she'd now have that tossed-about look that Amelia sported so effortlessly.

"How far is it to where we're going, Miss Earhart?" she asked.

"Call me Amelia. It's only in Burbank, just a few miles away. My friend, Paul Mantz, will let me use one of his planes. No one will bother us either."

"Does he have many?"

"I think he's up to six now." They sped past an intensely green golf course where hordes of people were playing, some-where among them, G.P. "Paul owns a charter-plane service. He's a stunt man for the moving pictures and a wonderful pilot. He taught my stepson David how to fly. He's also been a dear friend and mentor to me."

Lindsey noticed how animated Amelia was today. Maybe it was because no one was bossing her around or trying to get a piece of her. Lindsey desperately wanted to ask questions about her upcoming flight but sensed that might be an intrusion on the woman's happiness. She'd ask her questions later.

At the United Airport, Lindsey and T.J. met Paul Mantz. He was every inch a Hollywood stunt-pilot-type—dapper, handsome, well-built, and just Amelia's height, five foot eight. He embraced Amelia, obviously delighted to see her.

"I thought I'd never see you again!" he joked playfully. "And here you are with two people I haven't met."

"Yes, I've escaped at last!" she squealed. "Paul Mantz, this is T.J. Wakesnoris, who will be with G.P. on the radio during my flight."

"Nice to meet you, Wakesnoris."

"I'm glad to meet you, as well, Mr. Mantz."

"Paul to you." He turned to Lindsey. "And who's this younger version of Amelia Earhart?" he asked, taking her hand and kissing it gallantly. She felt herself blushing.

"This is Lindsey, T.J.'s daughter. G.P. has dubbed her 'Amelia Two.'"

"I can see why," Mantz said. "The resemblance is striking indeed." He put his arm around Amelia's shoulders. "What brings you here today, darling?"

"I want to fly, to feel that wonderful freedom that made me turn to piloting in the first place," she said, hugging herself. "And I want my friends to enjoy it with me."

"Sounds good to me. Now, then, which of the planes do you prefer, Amelia? As if I don't know!" He poked her arm.

"The Vega, of course," she said with a grin.

"This woman loves the Vega," Mantz told T.J. and Lindsey, "the quirkiest plane I think I've ever seen! You can only take one person up at a time, though. It's not big enough for three."

"Sure it is," Amelia said.

"Honey, it's a tight enough squeeze with two, let alone three." Mantz's tone was no longer teasing.

"I'll be glad to wait my turn," T.J. said.

"Don't you want to go?" Lindsey asked.

"Well, uh, sure, but I can wait if there's not enough room."

Lindsey recalled T.J.'s airsickness on their flight to Hawaii. Maybe this wasn't the best idea after all—for him at least.

"Nonsense, we'll all fit," Amelia was saying.

Mantz shook his head. "The lady wants to go up. What more can I say? Give me a few minutes, and I'll get a Vega ready for you."

The tiny plane was made largely of wood. Lindsey tingled with excitement as she watched Amelia, Paul Mantz, and one of his employees prepare the Vega for takeoff.

"Would you rather not go?" Lindsey asked T.J. at one point. He seemed nervous, constantly jiggling the loose change in his pants pocket.

"Actually, I wouldn't."

"That's okay. I think she'll understand."

T.J. shook his head. "I'm not so sure about that. After all, she gets airsick, too, but she keeps going up."

"You don't think she'll get sick today, do you?" That would be pretty gross.

"Who knows?"

"Well, we're all set," Amelia said, striding confidently toward them.

Lindsey glanced at her teacher. Was he going or not?

"Amelia, if you don't mind, I think I'll wait this one out," T.J. said.

"Really? It's quite safe. Paul's just a worrywart."

"Nevertheless, the thought of going up in that makes me queasy."

"Now here is a sensible person," Paul Mantz said. "I'll show you around the airfield while the girls take their joyride."

Amelia patted T.J.'s arm. "That's fine. C'mon, Lindsey. Let's show them what we women can do!"

Mantz boosted Lindsey into the small cockpit. Amelia followed, then strapped them in before starting up the thunderous engines.

"Ready?" Amelia shouted over the roar.

"Ready!" Lindsey gave her thumbs up.

The aviatrix started down the runway, picking up speed as she went. Lindsey felt her back press against the seat, and she held on tightly as the Vega bumped and lurched upon takeoff.

"Weeee!" she shouted. "This is great!" Lindsey waved at T.J. and Paul Mantz, who were watching.

"Doing okay?" Amelia asked.

"Yes! I love it!"

For the next two hours Lindsey felt like one enormous goose bump. To be flying with the legendary Amelia Earhart was the stuff of which impossible dreams were made. Nothing in her life had ever thrilled her more than this.

They flew over the ocean, then curved inland and swept past the San Bernardino Mountains and the Palm Springs desert. It was a rough ride; they tossed about on the air currents, but Lindsey had a strong stomach and enjoyed every minute of her adventure. She knew the jarring flight would probably have made T.J. sick. She didn't think Ben would've liked it either.

Lindsey wished the flight would go on and on. When the gas gauge inched closer and closer toward empty, however, Amelia announced it was time to take the Vega in. The plane skidded hard, then surged upward once before landing. Still, Lindsey's joy bubbled over. A waiting Paul Mantz helped her out of the cockpit.

"I see she got you back in one piece," he joked. "You had me worried there for a minute." He pointed to his head. "See these gray hairs? Amelia Earhart is the reason behind every one of them."

"Oh, I loved it!" Lindsey clapped her hands. "I want to be a pilot someday."

"Uh-oh." Mantz smacked his hand lightly against his high forehead. "Now look what you've done, Amelia." He turned to T.J. "I hope you have a fat bank account."

T.J. grinned sheepishly. "Lindsey does have a way of making her dreams come true."

They ate greasy hamburgers and tough french fries at the airfield's eatery, but to Lindsey, it was like ambrosia. On the way back to the Toluca Lake base, Lindsey decided it was time to put some questions to Amelia.

"Amelia, may I ask you some things about your next flight?" Lindsey asked uncertainly. But when the woman stiffened, she quickly added, "Or would you rather not?" The last thing she wanted to do was offend her hero.

"I guess it would be okay."

"I won't if you'd rather not."

Amelia roughed up Lindsey's hair. "Go ahead, Two." On

the flight, she'd taken to calling Lindsey just plain "Two," rather than "Amelia Two." Lindsey loved it.

"When will you be leaving?"

Amelia hesitated. "I'm not exactly sure, but it should be within the next few weeks. I've always hated to say when I'll be leaving on a major flight. I don't like being accused of publicity-seeking—or cowardice, if the flight is canceled." She sighed. "Reporters have been both wonderful and awful to me."

"How long will the flight last?"

"Somewhere around four to five weeks. G.P. wants me back for the Fourth of July." She laughed wryly, then took on the demeanor of a radio announcer. "Amelia Earhart, All-American patriot, returns from her record-breaking around-the-world-trip!"

Lindsey and T.J. laughed.

"Will you go to Hawaii first?" Lindsey asked.

"Not this time."

"Really? Why not?"

"Well, there's a seasonal shift in wind patterns," Amelia said carefully.

Lindsey could tell she was holding back. She'd just ask T.J. for more details later. "You won't be alone, will you?" she asked.

Amelia shook her head as she stopped for some pedestrians. "I'm taking a navigator, Fred Noonan. I guess you haven't met him yet. Have you, T.J.?"

"Just once when I was out and about. He seems very capable."

"He is," Amelia said.

Why wasn't Lindsey convinced? "Where will the boys and

I stay while T.J. monitors the radio?"

Amelia looked surprised. "At my house, of course. My mother, Mrs. DeCarrie, and Margot can look after you."

"I guess that's safe?" Lindsey blurted before she could stop herself.

"Excuse me?" Amelia looked puzzled.

In their past two adventures, Lindsey, T.J., and the boys had had to be together when they traveled back to their own time. What would happen if T.J. wasn't with them?

"The Lord has a way of working these things out," T.J. said cryptically, calming her fears.

Amelia laughed awkwardly. "Yes, he does, doesn't he?"

"You believe in him, then?" Lindsey said quickly.

"Of course," Amelia replied.

Lindsey was about to investigate further the depth of Amelia Earhart's commitment to God, but just then a dog ran into the street. Amelia slammed on the brakes, and Lindsey thrust her hands against the dashboard to keep herself from being propelled through the windshield. She felt T.J. bump into the back of her seat.

"So sorry!" Amelia called out. "Is everyone all right?"

They assured her that they were. Fortunately the little beagle had made it to safety.

"I'm positively daft when it comes to braking for animals," Amelia admitted. "G.P. gets so mad at me sometimes. He's afraid I'll kill myself trying to avoid some stray, but I just can't seem to help myself. I'm terribly sorry to have scared you like that."

"It's okay," Lindsey said.

The opportunity to talk about faith seemed lost, at least for the moment. Just before they arrived at the Putnam house, however, Lindsey danced around its edges. "Amelia, are you ever afraid to fly?"

The aviatrix thought about that for a few moments as the wind wreaked havoc with her short hair. "Not terribly," she said finally. "You know, Two, the only thing that scares me is the prospect of going down in an African jungle. But then I don't plan for that to happen, dear." She threw a charming smile in Lindsey's direction.

"It sounds like you've weighed all the consequences, Amelia," T.J. said.

"Yes, I have. I love life, and that means taking risks. As far as I know, I've only got one obsession—a small and probably feminine horror of growing old—so I won't feel completely cheated if I fail to come back."

Chapter Seven

Just after Amelia pulled the Cord Phaeton into the driveway, another vehicle slid in beside them. The pilot scrunched her eyes to identify the driver and lit up when she saw who it was.

"Walter!" She hopped out of the car and hurried toward the man, but just then Mrs. DeCarrie appeared in the back doorway.

"Amelia!" she called. "That photographer is here. He's been waiting for an hour."

Amelia groaned, and her shoulders slumped. "Good night! I completely forgot about him."

As the man named Walter came closer, G.P. slipped past Mrs. DeCarrie and took his wife by the arm, steering her toward the house. "C'mon, Amelia, Baruch's waiting, too. You look refreshed. Where were you?"

"Out flying," she said without enthusiasm. "Come, T.J., it's back to work for us."

"Thank you, Amelia," Lindsey called after them. "I had a wonderful time."

"You're welcome, Two."

"Walter McMenamy!" Mrs. DeCarrie looked happy to see the man.

"Hello, Mrs. DeCarrie," he said, approaching the house. "Maybe I should come back at another time."

McMenamy. McMenamy. Where had Lindsey heard that name before? Ah, yes! Mrs. DeCarrie had mentioned that he used to be a regular at the house, but seldom came around anymore.

"No, you don't." She led him toward the backyard patio where a pool shimmered in the early afternoon sun. "You stay right here, and I'll bring some lemonade. Lindsey, this is Mr. McMenamy. He's Miss Earhart's radio man, or whatever his official title is. Will you keep him company?"

"Sure!" Any opportunity to learn more about her hero's flight was just fine with Lindsey.

He held open a wooden gate, and Lindsey went over to some white wrought-iron garden furniture. They sat under an arbor of orange trees which gave off a sweetly pungent fragrance.

"I'm Lindsey Wakesnoris," she said, relieved not to have messed up her last name for once.

Suddenly her brother and Ben showed up.

"Mrs. DeCarrie said you just got back!" Ben's eyes were wide behind his glasses. "Did you actually fly with Amelia Earhart?"

"Yes, I did." Lindsey laughed with the sheer pleasure of it all.

"Too bad we slept in," Andrew said with remorse. "I would have loved it."

"Not me," Ben said.

"Not T.J.—" She quickly glanced at McMenamy— "Uh, Dad, either." Lindsey laughed again. "Not when he saw how small the Vega was. That's the plane Amelia took me up in." She turned then to Mr. McMenamy. "Uh, guys, I'm just meeting

Mr. Walter McMenamy. This is my brother, Andrew, and my cous—my other brother, Ben."

"Nice to meet you, sir," the boys each said.

"The pleasure's mine," McMenamy replied. "Please have a seat."

The heavy chairs scraped noisily against the concrete patio.

"Mr. McMenamy is a radio technician for Amelia," Lindsey said.

"So, it's Amelia now, is it?" Andrew teased.

"So, it is!" She smiled, full of joy. She felt comfortable with Mr. McMenamy. For one thing, Mrs. DeCarrie had spoken so highly of him. For another, he had the nicest face—sort of round and boyish. Lindsey wondered how old he was.

"I hear your father will be manning the radio with G.P. in San Francisco," McMenamy said.

"That's right."

Mrs. DeCarrie appeared then, carrying a rather heavy-looking tray of lemonade, glasses, and cookies. Walter McMenamy shot up from his chair to take it from her. He set it carefully on the table. "Won't you join us, Mrs. D.?" he said.

She giggled like a junior-high girl at a slumber party. "Why I'd love to, for as long as no one needs me inside, that is."

He held out a chair for her, and Mrs. DeCarrie slipped into it. Then she poured an icy glass of lemonade for everyone.

"Where are you from?" McMenamy said, turning back to Lindsey and the boys.

"Virginia," Andrew said around a mouthful of oatmeal cookie. He hadn't learned yet not to speak and eat at the same time.

"That's quite a distance. How do you like California?"

"I love it," Lindsey said fervently. She took a long sip of lemonade, relishing its coolness, feeling pulp sticking to her lips.

"And you flew with Amelia? What a wonderful experience that must have been for you!"

"Oh, it was!" Lindsey then launched into a full-blown description of her flying adventure with the legendary Amelia Earhart.

When she finished, Mrs. DeCarrie said, "That's something to tell your children."

"And my children's children," Lindsey said, quoting from the Bible.

"And how have you been, Walter?" Mrs. DeCarrie asked after a pause.

The question seemed to eclipse his joy. "I'm okay," he answered carefully.

"We don't see you around here much anymore. Not since the crash."

"I know." The drink in his hand trembled.

"Mr. McMenamy was Miss Earhart's radio operator on her first attempt to fly around the world," the housekeeper said. "And will be again this time, won't you, Walter?"

"Yes, I will." He became thoughtful as if wondering how to say something. "I'll be joined by a number of others this time, however. Such as your father." He nodded at the children.

"Will you be with him in San Francisco?" Lindsey asked.

The dark-haired man shook his head. "No. I'll be at a hook-up not too far from here. My job is to relay information to the press."

"That sounds interesting."

McMenamy sniffed. "It certainly will be."

Lindsey wondered what that was all about.

"How does that radio contact work?" Ben asked.

"Mother!" Margot DeCarrie called from the kitchen window. "I need you!"

Mrs. DeCarrie rose slowly from her chair. When McMenamy also got up, the boys followed his example. "I'm wanted." She leaned over and kissed McMenamy's cheek. "I'm so glad you came. Don't be such a stranger."

He smiled. "You're a gem among women."

After Mrs. DeCarrie left, McMenamy began to explain how the radio hook-up on the Electra 10-E worked.

"Is that the name of Amelia's plane?" Lindsey asked.

"That's right," he said. "We refer to the radio system that keeps us in contact with Amelia as DF equipment, which stands for direction finding."

"What's it look like?" Lindsey asked.

McMenamy grinned sheepishly and pulled out his wallet. "I just happen to have a picture of it." He showed them a black-and-white photo of him and Amelia Earhart standing next to the Lockheed Electra 10-E. They all huddled closer to see it. "If you look on top of the plane's body, or fuselage," he said, "you'll see an antenna mounted there."

"Oh yeah, I see it," Lindsey said.

The boys nodded after they located it.

"Then there are wires leading back to the vertical tail fins." He traced this with his finger. "It's very heavy, about four-hundred pounds of wire."

"That sounds pretty clumsy," Lindsey said.

"Lindsey!"

"What? What did I say, Ben?"

"It just sounded well, rude, you know."

"I'm sorry, Mr. McMenamy. I didn't mean to be rude."

"I didn't think you were," McMenamy said kindly, "but thanks anyway. The truth is, the DF equipment is very cumbersome. The antenna isn't only heavy, it's long, 250 feet long."

"Wow!" the Dreamers said.

"There are also some simple radios in the cockpit for voice and Morse code communication."

"I'm wondering how Amelia and her nalligator will talk to each other in the plane," Andrew said. "I heard they don't sit too close to each other."

"Nalligator?" McMenamy looked confused.

"He means navigator," Lindsey said quickly, not wanting to draw attention to her brother's dyslexia.

Andrew blushed. "I get letters mixed up sometimes," he said.

"That's okay." McMenamy reassured him. "Actually that's a good question, Andrew. Fred, as in Noonan, the navigator, will sit in the back of the plane at a table. He'll have maps and compasses to help him, well, navigate the flight. It's noisy from the engines inside the 10-E, so rather than shout at each other, they have a special system worked out." He laughed. "It's simply a bamboo fishing rod for passing messages back and forth."

Lindsey thought that sounded primitive, but she knew better than to say so.

"What do they eat when they're up there?" Ben asked, getting into one of his favorite subjects.

"Very little, I'm afraid. Amelia usually gets airsick, so she sticks to hard-boiled eggs and tomato juice. As for Noonan—"

"What does he eat?" Andrew asked, pressing for an answer.

"He usually drinks his meals," McMenamy said with an edge to his usually-pleasant voice.

Lindsey exchanged knowing looks with the boys.

"What's Mr. Noonan like?" Ben asked.

"Let's see," McMenamy said. "He's in his mid-forties, tall, slim, Irish. Served in the Royal Navy during World War I. Spent over twenty years at sea in His Majesty's service. Quite an adventurer really."

"How so?" Andrew asked.

"He went around Cape Horn a number of times, which is a nasty stretch of water. After his career with the navy, Noonan became a pilot for Pan American Airways."

"Is that what he does now?" Lindsey asked.

McMenamy shook his head and looked uneasy. "He got fired for excessive drinking."

This worried Lindsey. "Should he be Amelia's navigator, then?"

"Some don't think so. Amelia's convinced he's okay now."

"Are you?"

"Let's just hope Amelia's right, Lindsey," he said.

McMenamy checked his watch, then rose from the table. "I'd better get going."

Lindsey wondered if they'd asked too many questions. They walked him to his car and waved him off.

"That was really interesting," Andrew said as the car drove away.

"It sure was!" Ben replied. "I just hope we didn't put him off."

"He did seem a little uncomfortable," Lindsey said. "But at

least we learned a lot more."

"Too bad about that Noonan guy," Ben said. "He sounds like bad news."

"Yeah," Lindsey agreed. "Well, I'm going back to the patio to clean up. Mrs. DeCarrie seems really busy today."

"Want some help?" Ben asked.

"Sure."

They wandered back to the patio and began collecting glasses, napkins, and the few cookies the boys hadn't eaten.

"Say, what's this?" Lindsey said as she spotted the photo of Walter McMenamy and Amelia Earhart sticking out from under a napkin.

"He forgot it," Ben said.

"I'll just keep it until I see him again." Lindsey slid it carefully into her pocket. "I'll put it in my purse and give it to him later."

Ben carried the tray into the kitchen. Lindsey and Andrew washed the glasses and other dishes and put away the extra lemonade and cookies. Lindsey headed to her room then, but the sound of Amelia Earhart's voice stopped her on the top step. The door to the Putnams' bedroom at the end of the hall was ajar, and the couple was talking loudly.

"I need to, G.P.," Amelia was saying. "This pressure is getting terrible."

"Can't you hold out a few more days?" he pleaded.

"No. If I'm not only going to make but survive this crazy flight, I have to do some things my way."

"Where will you be?"

"The Cochrans'," Amelia answered.

"Why them?"

"Because Jackie is a dear friend who will let me relax to my heart's content."

"Must you do this?" G.P. asked.

"If you want me to fly around the world, I must," Amelia said firmly.

"Then I guess it's settled," G.P. said in resignation.

Chapter Eight

Lindsey compared the next four weeks to riding on a bus. Just when it was rolling along at a nice pace, it stopped. Then it started again. Then it stopped. Start. Stop. Start. Stop.

Amelia Earhart had gone to her friend's house to rest before flying around the world. Only once during that time did Lindsey get to see her. Mrs. DeCarrie took her, the boys, and a suitcase full of clothes and books to the Cochrans' beautiful estate. Lindsey thought her hero looked refreshed, the school-girl side beaming through. She was glad to see Amelia in good spirits. She'd have to be to attempt such a dangerous flight.

Their time together passed too quickly. Lindsey only got to spend an hour with Amelia Earhart before it was time to head back to Hollywood and homework. In the context of the spring of 1937, Lindsey and the boys would have been in school. As it was, Mrs. DeCarrie made sure they "kept up with their lessons." But all Lindsey wanted to learn about now was Amelia's plane and navigator and communications system.

On May 1 Margot DeCarrie entered the den where Lindsey and the boys were working on a math assignment T.J. had given them. She brandished a glossy magazine.

"I thought you especially might like to see this, Lindsey."

She took the magazine and gasped. Amelia's face beamed from the cover of *McCall's*. The caption read, "America's Great

Women: Amelia Earhart, Who Spanned an Ocean and Won a World." Ben and Andrew peeked over Lindsey's shoulder.

"This is wonderful!" Lindsey leafed through the magazine to find the story about Amelia. "May I read this, Margot?"

"That was the general idea." After a pause she said dreamily, "And so it begins."

"What begins?" asked Ben. "Is Amelia ready to fly?"

The boys had confided in Lindsey that they, too, were growing restless from the wait.

"I think she'll be ready soon," Margot said, "but I'm actually referring to public relations. G.P. is at the top of his game right now, promoting Amelia and her flight. That's why you haven't seen him around much lately."

Andrew shrugged. "I just figured he was with Amelia at her friend's house."

"Not on your life. He's been hustling wire services, radio stations, newspapers, magazines, and so forth. He set up a book contract for Amelia to tell the story of her flight. She even went to New York for a couple of days to promote philatelic covers for the flight at a department store."

"What are phi-phi…" Andrew gave it up.

"Philatelic," Margot said effortlessly. "Stamps. She'll be carrying first-day-of-issue stamps on the plane. When she returns from her flight with them, they'll be worth a small fortune. Another of G.P.'s schemes."

"When is she coming home?" asked Lindsey.

"I guess it will take some weeks to make the flight."

Lindsey shook her head. "No, I mean come home here."

"Tomorrow."

"I can't wait to see her again!"

"Don't count on being with her much, Lindsey. She'll be busy-busy until the trip begins. From now on, you'll see lots more of reporters than you'll see of Amelia." She sighed. "And that phone will be ringing off the hook." As if to emphasize that remark, the phone in her office rang. "Just as I was saying." She grinned wryly and left the Dreamers.

Lindsey became thoughtful. "You know, guys, I haven't seen that William Miller around here lately."

"Didn't you know?" Ben asked.

"Know what?" Lindsey hated it when her cousin or brother knew something she didn't.

"I heard T.J. say he had to leave the country on another assignment."

"Isn't that strange?"

Ben shook his head. "I don't think so. T.J. and that Mr. Baruch seem to be doing most of the work now."

Andrew scratched his head. "I never did understand who that Miller guy was."

"He was from the government," Lindsey said, "representing President Roosevelt—probably making sure Amelia knows what's expected of her on this flight."

"I wouldn't want to be in her shoes," Ben said.

"Why not?" Lindsey asked.

"As you well know, I'm not much of a traveler." Lindsey and Andrew twittered at this. "I can't imagine flying around the world in that plane. I know it's state of the art for 1937, but I doubt it would get cleared for takeoff in our time."

"Did you see how the metal outsides are pop-riveted

together?" Andrew asked in disbelief.

"Shake, rattle, and roll. Better her than me."

"Maybe not better her, either," Lindsey said darkly.

Margot DeCarrie's prediction proved correct. From the time Amelia returned home to the time she left on her flight, reporters, photographers, and other well-wishers mobbed the Toluca Lake house. A soldier was enlisted to prevent people from storming the place. Lindsey found it strange that the public didn't question this. But then she remembered T.J. saying how trusting Americans were in the 1930s. They wouldn't ever suspect that their government, not to mention Amelia Earhart, could be involved in spying.

On the night of May 19 Lindsey took forever to fall asleep. There was so much activity downstairs that the noise level and her keen interest in all of it kept her wide awake. Amelia would be ready to leave on her historic flight in a day or two; how could anyone sleep? Lindsey finally drifted off around three o'clock.

To her annoyance, it was ten o'clock when she awoke. The house was strangely quiet except for a bird at her window teasing her with its steady chirping. What if Amelia had left, and Lindsey wasn't able to say good-bye? The very thought made her stomach feel heavy, almost sick. She pushed back the covers, slipped into a bathrobe, and rushed to T.J.'s door. When the teacher didn't answer, Lindsey cautiously peeked inside. He wasn't there. She turned to go, but then spotted a note taped to the dresser mirror. Quickly, Lindsey snatched it and read, "The plane's in Burbank. Getting ready to roll."

"Oh, why didn't he wake me up?" She wondered if the boys were still in their room. Surely T.J. wouldn't have taken them and left her. Maybe they could find someone to drive them to the airport.

Lindsey rushed to the boys' room and knocked repeatedly. When she finally heard moans, her heart lifted, and she burst inside.

"You guys overslept, too!"

Ben sat up slowly. "Why not? We couldn't sleep last night with all that racket downstairs."

"What're you doing up so early?" Andrew rubbed his eyes.

"It's not early. It's ten o'clock, and T.J. left this note." She shoved it in front of Ben's nose. He reached for his glasses on the night table.

"Do you think she's leaving today?" he asked seconds later.

"Could be. I don't fully understand the note. But if she's starting out, we have to say good-bye." Lindsey's voice was a plea. "Hurry up and get dressed. Maybe we can get a ride to the airport from someone. I can't believe T.J. would do this to us!"

With the speed of a racer Lindsey rushed to her room. In a blur of arms and legs she selected an attractive pair of loose-fitting pants, a short, military-type jacket, and of course, the ever-present scarf Amelia had given her. She knew Mrs. DeCarrie wouldn't approve. The housekeeper had bought Lindsey a number of dresses, but Lindsey only had eyes for Amelia's aviator clothing, especially today.

She hurried downstairs and heard a loud whistle coming from the kitchen. The tea kettle was boiling over! Where was Mrs. DeCarrie? Lindsey rushed into the kitchen where she found Mrs. Earhart calmly taking cookies out of a tin. The nearly deaf woman couldn't hear the piercing noise. Lindsey moved swiftly to the kettle and lifted it from the electric burner, then turned off the heat.

"Oh, hello, Lindsey," Mrs. Earhart said calmly. "Is it ready so soon?"

"Yes."

"Would you like a cup of tea?"

"No, thank you. Where is Mrs. DeCarrie?"

"Huh?"

Lindsey tried again, slower and louder. "Where is Mrs. DeCarrie?"

"Shopping."

How could she be shopping at a time like this? "Where is everyone else?"

"What's that?" Mrs. Earhart cupped a hand to her ear.

"I said, where is everyone else?" This could take forever, and she didn't have forever. *Lord, please help me be patient.*

"They all left."

"Where to?"

"Huh?"

"Where to?" Lindsey's voice cracked from shouting.

"I don't know."

Nor did Mrs. Earhart know how to drive. Who, then, could take Lindsey and the boys to Burbank? The guard wouldn't leave his post. Maybe the gardener! He was usually around. Lindsey thanked Mrs. Earhart and headed for the back door. At that moment someone pulled into the driveway. Walter McMenamy!

She bolted out the door. "Mr. McMenamy!"

"Lindsey! Is something wrong?" His dark eyes held a hint of alarm.

Suddenly the boys appeared, racing to keep up with Lindsey. They panted hasty greetings to the radio technician.

"Our dad left a note saying that everyone's with the plane in Burbank. I'm afraid they'll leave without us."

A shadow passed over McMenamy's boyish face. "Thanks for telling me," he muttered. Seconds later he announced, "Let's go!"

"Excuse me?" Had Lindsey heard him correctly?

"We're going to Burbank. Hop in the car!"

Lindsey ran back to tell Mrs. Earhart where they were going, then grabbed her purse and followed the boys into McMenamy's car.

McMenamy drove as fast as the speed limit allowed to the Burbank airport. He parked vertically in a diagonal spot, and they poured out of the car like gum balls from a vending machine.

"There's the plane!" Lindsey pointed toward the lustrous Lockheed Electra 10-E. "She hasn't left yet!"

A cordon of military guards surrounded the plane, protecting it from the journalists. Several yards away a few select reporters pressed around T.J. and G.P., begging to know when Miss Earhart was going to leave. Lindsey and the boys walked over to hear what was being said while Walter McMenamy rushed off in a different direction. G.P. was busy explaining that the flight around the world was not about to start just yet.

"She's going to take a quick run up to Oakland," he yelled above the clamor of other planes taking off and landing.

Lindsey met T.J.'s gaze, and they waved at each other.

"When will she leave for the trip?" a tow-headed reporter asked.

"We'll keep you boys informed," G.P. answered.

As G.P. droned on, Lindsey went in search of Walter, the boys tagging along after her. As they passed the plane, Lindsey noticed something odd. The direction-finding equipment Walter McMenamy had told them about was not in place. Lindsey suddenly remembered the photo he had left behind. She quickly fished it out of her purse and compared it to the plane on the runway.

"What's up?" Andrew asked.

"I'm not sure just yet." She continued scanning the photo. There were the direction-finding antenna and wire. And there was another thing. When Lindsey had first seen the Electra at the military air base, there were no markings on it. Now there were. Emblazoned on the plane's wings and tail was "NR 16020." And what were those strange pieces of equipment just underneath the plane? Could they be hidden cameras?

Now Lindsey understood why the guards were needed to prevent the handful of reporters from getting closer. Even if they got too close, however, would the journalists notice anything amiss? This was 1937, after all. The public trusted its officials. This was beyond Lindsey, of course. In her time Americans—especially reporters—questioned leaders all the time.

Discreetly, Lindsey pointed out to the boys what she had discovered.

"I can't believe no one else can see this stuff," Andrew whispered.

"Me neither."

"Hey, you kids!" shouted an irate man in mechanics overalls. "Git away from here! Go on. Git!"

Chapter Nine

They scurried off like mice being chased by a determined cat.

Lindsey spotted Paul Mantz standing near the airport office, looking like he was ready to fly. "Hey! That's Amelia's friend. He's the guy who got our plane ready the other day. It looks like Walter McMenamy knows him, too," Lindsey said, as she watched the two men greet each other. "Let's go talk to them. T.J. looks too busy for us right now."

"Well, if it isn't Amelia Two!" the wiry Paul Mantz greeted her. He'd been smoking and dropped his cigarette to the ground now, stepping lightly on it.

Lindsey was thrilled that he remembered her and her nickname. She quickly introduced the boys, noting that although genial, Mantz's expression was strained. For the next few moments, he and McMenamy spoke as if it were just the two of them there.

"Yeah, I'm going to Oakland with her today," Mantz said. "It's a publicity thing G.P.'s doing. But I'm telling you now, that plane isn't ready. That radio system of hers doesn't have a strong enough frequency for this journey."

"I know what you mean. I kept telling G.P., but he wouldn't listen, and he wouldn't let me near Amelia. Maybe you can convince her how important that is."

"I can try, but she hardly listens to me," Mantz said. "And

you know, even if the direction-finding equipment were in order, she needs more time to go over fuel consumption with me. I keep trying to tell her she needs more training, but she keeps right on refusing it. As if that weren't enough, she still doesn't know telegraphic code well enough for this flight." He shook his head and clucked his tongue. "She's such a romantic about flight. She doesn't have time for the nitty-gritty parts of it."

"Yeah, she's always been that way," McMenamy agreed. "Remember her Hawaii to Oakland flight in '35?"

"I certainly do!"

"What happened?" Lindsey blurted.

"Amelia used the radio to listen to music and weather and talk to G.P.," McMenamy said. "The crews of four Coast Guard cutters couldn't make contact with her because she didn't give them any position reports. If you plan to fly, young lady, don't take after her in that respect." He lowered his voice as he turned back to Mantz, and Lindsey strained to hear. "I wonder if old Noonan knows more than we do, or if he's as much in the dark as we are."

Lindsey followed their gazes to a tall, distinguished-looking man in a suit and felt hat. He stood with his hands in his pockets, self-assured. Was this navigator Fred Noonan?

Paul Mantz threw his hands up. "Who knows!"

"I sure don't. Those government men keep shoving me aside. I didn't even know she was going to Oakland today, Paul. That's how much they tell me. There's a lot more here than meets the eye."

Mantz nodded somberly. They were all silent then. At least some people were questioning all the weird parts of this flight.

Lindsey had begun to wonder if everyone wasn't being just plain dumb about the obvious. She heard Mantz make a thwipping noise with his teeth. "I just hope she knows what she's doing," he said.

G.P. kept up a steady stream of chatter at dinner that night, but the heavy mood was so thick not even a plane's propeller could cut through it. Not so for the beef tenderloin. It fell into delicious bites with little more than a tap from Lindsey's fork. She'd never tasted meat so good. She noticed Amelia merely toying with her food, but everyone else at the table—G.P., T.J., Andrew, Ben, Mrs. DeCarrie, Margot DeCarrie, Mrs. Amy Earhart, and Bernard Baruch—were digging in.

"Amelia, you must eat!" Mrs. DeCarrie scolded. "You'll be existing on hard-boiled eggs and tomato juice for the next few weeks—when you're lucky. In those God-forsaken countries you'll land in, who knows what you'll find!"

Amelia grasped the housekeeper by the hand and smiled sweetly at her. "Dear Mrs. DeCarrie. Always concerned about her Amelia."

"Your mother is, too." Mrs. DeCarrie gestured with her head toward the older woman. Amy Earhart appeared not to hear. She stared at her plate, keeping her thoughts private.

"Please don't worry about me," Amelia said. "I'm fine. I ate like a horse in Oakland today at a reception. If I fill my stomach tonight, I may be sicker than usual tomorrow."

Lindsey straightened up. "Are you leaving tomorrow?"

Amelia looked at G.P. before answering. He closed his eyes and nodded. "Yes, Lindsey, but few people know about it."

"I thought maybe you were leaving today."

"The Oakland flight was a trial run for the plane, what we call a shakedown flight. We wanted to make sure everything was working."

Ben quickly swallowed a mouthful of baked potato, then asked, "Was it?"

"I'm happy to say it was." Amelia seemed more cheerful as she discussed the flight openly.

"Amelia, I was just wondering, why doesn't the press know about your plans to leave tomorrow?" Lindsey hoped she wasn't crossing a line here.

The woman hesitated, then explained, "Lindsey, pilots are a bit funny about making such announcements. I always have been anyway. In the fullness of time things are ready to talk about, not before."

Lindsey thought she understood. "You mean, like if something had gone wrong today, the reporters might get the wrong impression about the plane or the safety of your attempt to go around the world?"

Amelia smiled. "Exactly."

"But everything's okay?" Andrew pressed.

"Yes, dear Andrew, everything's okay."

Lindsey thought she saw tears in Mrs. Earhart's eyes. But the woman couldn't hear that well. Maybe Amelia had taken her mother aside privately before dinner to tell her she was leaving.

"Where will you go first?" Lindsey asked.

"Miami. This will give me an opportunity to test the Electra over a longer dis—"

G.P. sat forward. "If there's anything wrong that would threaten an around-the-world flight, we can come back to

Burbank and take care of it here. That's why we want to make sure the reporters don't get too excited until we actually leave."

Lindsey was puzzled. "You're going, too, G.P.?" She had thought Amelia was taking only her navigator, Fred Noonan.

G.P. laughed. "Actually, I'll be joining Amelia for the first leg, another flight to Oakland. It'll be me, Amelia, Noonan, and our mechanic."

"You're not going anywhere, are you, Dad?" Lindsey asked anxiously.

"Yes, I'll be going to the Beacon Hill station, receiving transmissions from the Electra." He mouthed silently, "Not to worry."

But she would worry. It was one thing to have T.J. a few minutes away, another thing entirely to have him a few hours away. She did, after all, want to get back to her own time when this adventure ended.

"When I know everything's all right," G.P. went on, "I'll go to Beacon Hill and stay with T.J. at the radio."

Bernard Baruch finally spoke up. "Tell me, Amelia, what do you plan to do for an encore?"

Her expression became thoughtful. "I think I have one good flight in me, this one. Afterwards I'd like to fly just for fun and for my public appearances."

Sadly, Lindsey knew there would be no encore.

Amelia's appetite seemed to improve the more she talked about the flight. She ate a large piece of double fudge chocolate cake and washed it down with a tall glass of milk. Then, getting up from the table, she said, "T.J., could I see you in the den for a while? There are some last minute details I want to go over with you."

"Sure."

"I promise it won't take long. We all need a good night's sleep."

Lindsey felt her pulse race. She had a sudden idea, although she didn't know how it would go over with Amelia or G.P.

"Uh, Amelia?" she asked hesitantly.

"Yes, Two?" Amelia said as she playfully roughed up Lindsey's hair.

"I was just wondering. Could we all have a prayer together? I mean, to ask God to just, well, be with you on your flight and everything."

For a moment, Amelia Earhart gaped. Then she said, "What an excellent idea! G.P., why didn't you think of that?"

G.P. snorted. "Indeed! Me? Prayer?" He thumped his chest with a forefinger. Then he became serious. "It is a good idea, Lindsey. Who will do it, though? We aren't exactly religious people."

"I'd be happy to, G.P.," T.J. offered.

They all gathered in the comfortable, ivory-colored living room, settling down on the sprawling couch and matching stuffed chairs.

"Let's pray," T.J. said, and Lindsey took the boys' hands. Soon everyone was forming a circle and holding hands.

"Father in heaven," T.J. said, "we thank you for Amelia Earhart's courage in embarking on this great adventure. We ask that you would give your angels charge of her and Fred Noonan, to guard them in all their ways. Make your presence very real to them as they travel."

Was it silly for them to pray about a flight whose end was

already determined? Lindsey wondered. No, Amelia would find strength in the prayer and in God's presence. And really, the most important thing was Amelia's relationship with the Lord. Lindsey wanted to remind her that God was with her wherever she went, in the air or on the ground.

"Please help Amelia not to experience airsickness," T.J. was saying, "and may her dealings with Fred Noonan be positive. May all they do on this flight honor you and your Son, Jesus, in whose name we pray. Amen."

It was silent for a few moments. Then Amelia finally said, "Thank you, T.J., I really appreciate that."

On a sudden impulse, Lindsey unclasped the cross around her neck and handed it to Amelia. "I'd be really honored if you would take this with you," she said. "It will remind you that God is with you wherever you go."

"Oh, Lindsey, how sweet of you!" She took the cross and immediately put it around her neck. Then she untied her yellow silk scarf and draped it around Lindsey's neck.

"Thank you, Amelia!"

The aviatrix kissed her on the cheek, then took her by the shoulders. "The scarf will remind you of how much I think of you. But remember, darling Lindsey, don't try to *be* me. There's only one me." Lindsey felt embarrassed then—until Amelia added, "And there's just one you. Be yourself, and you'll honor the God who made us both."

It was a lesson Lindsey would never forget.

Chapter Ten

O h, come on, Andrew, you're hogging the paper!"
Lindsey made a grab for the front page of the Los
Angeles Times. She was dying to read its account of
Amelia Earhart's historic flight. Andrew, however, quickly
jerked the paper away from her.

"Just a minute, Lindsey! I'm almost finished."

"Ben, can't you do something?" Lindsey pleaded with her
cousin, who sat calmly munching on hot cinnamon toast.

Ben shrugged. "He's *your* brother."

Impatiently, Lindsey tapped her foot on the kitchen's tile
floor. Just as she was about to scream with frustration, Andrew
thrust the paper across the breakfast table.

"There!"

"Careful! You'll get eggs all over it." Lindsey wrinkled her
nose at a small yellow blob at the bottom of the front page.

Andrew mimicked her by wagging his head back and
forth.

"C'mon, y'all," Ben said. "I'd like to eat my breakfast in
peace."

Andrew nodded. "You're right, Ben. Sorry for, as you say,
'hogging,' Lindsey."

She lowered the paper until she could see Andrew over the
top. "Me, too. I shouldn't have snapped at you."

"Well! I wish my children had gotten along so well." Mrs.

DeCarrie was at the sink scouring a frying pan.

"I thought you just had Margot," Ben said.

She shook her head. "I also have two sons."

Lindsey wasn't paying attention. She was intent on finding the article about Amelia's journey. She couldn't seem to locate it, though. "Andrew, where was that story, anyway?" she asked finally.

"Let me show you." He got up from the table, then came over to Lindsey, where he pointed out a measly editorial about Amelia at the bottom of the second page.

"Again?" she asked in disbelief. "This dinky little piece? I don't believe this! Amelia Earhart, the bravest woman in America, makes the most incredible attempt to cross the world, and the papers give her this!" Lindsey slapped the *Times* with the back of her hand. "What could be more important?"

"That," Ben said, pointing to a headline.

Lindsey turned the large pages awkwardly. The front page banner screamed: "Striking Steel Workers Clash with Chicago Police. Five Dead. Over 100 Injured."

"I guess that is pretty important," she said quietly. "But still, Amelia deserved at least a little space on the front page."

The situation did not improve the following day. As Lindsey scanned the paper at breakfast once again, she saw that the steel workers had been bumped from the banner position, but it now belonged to the American commoner Wallis Warfield Simpson. The day before the divorced woman had married the King of England.

"Say! Isn't he the guy we met in Scotland?" Ben asked.

"You met King Edward?" Mrs. DeCarrie asked in surprise.

"Well, I...uh...I..."

"We were in Scotland a few years back," Lindsey said, wanting to rescue him. "We saw the king when he visited the country."

"You kids certainly get around, don't you?"

"I guess we do. T.—uh—Dad, has a way of finding adventures." Lindsey bit her tongue. T.J. had once told the Dreamers to tell no one where they'd come from. "They'd want to know the future so they could change the past" T.J. had said. "We can't let that happen. We're just here to find out how a situation got resolved."

"*Dad* called from Beacon Hill last night and said we could go to the radio transmitting station here today if we finished our homework," Andrew said.

"I'll bet the reporters hanging around there are excited about Amelia." Lindsey jumped up, nearly spilling the remains of milk and soggy cornflakes in her bowl. "Let's get to our studies, guys. Mrs. DeCarrie, who will take us to the radio station?"

"Margot. She has to run some things over there today anyway."

"Is G.P. back yet?" Ben asked.

"If he is, I haven't seen him. Of course, whenever Amelia makes a special flight, G.P. usually isn't home much," she said. "He's always out there hustling reporters. He wants to make sure they give her good coverage."

"Well, they aren't yet," Lindsey said in disgust.

"Don't worry," Mrs. DeCarrie said. "G.P. will soon be going to New York City to arrange more publicity."

"Before or after he comes home?" Andrew asked.

The housekeeper admitted she wasn't sure.

Lindsey began to feel a bit more admiration for G.P. now. If it wasn't for him, after all, people wouldn't be as interested as they were in Amelia's flying.

By one o'clock the Dreamers had finished their English and science assignments. Margot made a few phone calls after lunch, and then they were off to the radio transmitting station in Los Angeles. At the entrance gate, a guard stopped their car. Margot presented an identification card G.P. had made for associates and family members, and the guard motioned them through.

Lindsey, wearing the scarf her hero had given her, marveled at the complex gadgetry that covered the walls inside. It looked state of the art for the 1930s but ancient by her own time's standards. She guessed that the same radio equipment that filled a room in 1937 might occupy the space of a computer chip sixty years later.

Lindsey immediately saw the youthful Walter McMenamy stationed on one side of the large room near another man. Both wore headsets, except when communicating with each other. Mr. McMenamy also removed his headset when briefing reporters who were working out of a special press room down the hall. In that room was a bank of telephones, and huge black manual typewriters populated several tables.

Navy guards kept the radio men separate from the press. In addition, a heavy-set lieutenant was constantly present in the transmitting room itself. Since he didn't seem to be doing any work that Lindsey could see, she figured he must be a sort of bouncer.

During the next six days Lindsey followed the daily progress of Amelia's flight from the transmitting station. Amelia and Fred Noonan had sped along the east coasts of Central and

South America, stopping each night at the private homes of presidents and high-ranking national officials. The flyers slept just five hours or so a night. Then they were up before dawn, ready to strike out again over vast expanses of land and water.

"How's Amelia doing?" was the first question Lindsey asked Walter McMenamy each afternoon when she and the boys arrived at the station. He would fill them in, then get T.J. on a special phone line from Beacon Hill so the Dreamers could speak with him.

On the sixth day the Dreamers arrived to find McMenamy's colleague briefing the press. Lindsey went up to McMenamy afterwards. "He didn't say much about Amelia. How is she today?"

He pursed his lips as she waited for his response. "She's doing okay." McMenamy glanced cautiously at the lieutenant standing across the room, then lowering his voice, he added, "Amelia's been feeling sick to her stomach."

"What's wrong?" Lindsey asked, concerned. "Is it the usual flight sickness she gets?"

"Probably. Unfortunately every time they refuel, gas fumes leak into the cabin, making it difficult for Amelia to breathe. On top of the noise level, those fumes are a real challenge."

"Is Fred Noonan doing all right?" Ben asked.

"He seems to be."

"How come we don't read about this in the papers?" Andrew asked. "Wouldn't the public be interested in Amelia's physical condition?"

McMenamy glanced at the navy officer. "There's a lot you don't read about in the papers," he whispered.

"Why not?" Andrew prodded. "Why don't you tell the

reporters so they can write about Amelia's health? That's really important stuff."

"Andrew, the public can't know everything that's happening here."

"Why not?"

The youthful-looking man sighed heavily. "I'd better get back to work."

He put his headphones on and turned his back on Lindsey and the boys. They went down the hall for a Coke, which came out of a weird-looking vending machine in a thick green bottle.

"Boy, was he testy!" Andrew took a long swig of soda.

"You were asking too many questions," Lindsey said. "I think the navy is only allowing Mr. McMenamy to tell the press certain things." She sat on a filing cabinet and swung her legs as she spoke. In the background rapid typing filled the air with its repetitive ticka-ticka-ticka.

"That's why the public never knew exactly what happened to her," Ben said.

"Say, y'all, do you think Mr. McMenamy and that guy with him know the whole story?" Andrew asked.

Lindsey shook her head. "Doubtful. They know something's up, but Mr. McMenamy doesn't act like he knows why Amelia has done or is doing certain things."

Andrew snickered. "Wouldn't the navy split a gut if they knew how much we know?"

Lindsey and Ben laughed, too. "Let's just make sure we act dumb about it, or we'll get in big trouble," she said.

"Who's in big trouble?"

The Dreamers jumped at the male voice. When they turned to see T.J., they all crowded around him.

"We didn't expect you," Lindsey said.

"Yeah, when did you get back here?" Ben asked.

"Just a few minutes ago. G.P. wants me to check things out on this end for a few days. Make sure everything's in working order."

"Boy, it's good to see you, T.J.," Andrew said.

"It sure is," Ben agreed. "Sometimes I worry that you'll solve the mystery when we're not there and leave without us."

"That won't happen," T.J. assured them. "I'm sure the Lord has all the details worked out." He turned to Lindsey. "Now, what's this about trouble?"

"I was saying we'd be in trouble if the navy knew that we know as much as we do." She paused and grinned. "Did that make sense?"

T.J. nodded and poured himself a cup of hot coffee from a huge pot. Lindsey found the smooth aroma pleasant. When her teacher didn't say anything, she pressed on.

"How much does Walter McMenamy know?"

"He knows just enough to cooperate when the navy censors his press statements. Y'all should know that Walter McMenamy is a deeply patriotic man. He's been told that Amelia is doing a special assignment for the government, that it's in the best interests of national security." T.J. gingerly sipped the hot coffee as the Dreamers listened attentively. "He has sworn secrecy about not revealing confidential information."

"I knew there was a reason I liked him." Lindsey was pleased with herself. "He just seems like a person you can count on to do the right thing."

"In view of that, don't give him a hard time," T.J. said. "If you have questions, come to me with them." He paused. "So, do you have questions?"

"I'm unclear about something," Andrew said. "Does Mr. McMenamy get to talk to Amelia?"

"No. He can hear radio transmissions, but it's just one-way. G.P., a Coast Guard official, and I are the only ones who can get direct messages and even that's not all the time."

"What's it really like for her out there?" Lindsey asked. "Mr. McMenamy said she's been feeling nauseated."

"The conditions are rough, very rough. She flies for hours and hours, sometimes bucking strong headwinds and storms. And Walter's right—her stomach does keep rebelling. On the other hand, Amelia has successfully completed a fourth of the trip. That's around four-thousand miles."

"Why don't the papers write more about her?" Ben asked. "Lindsey's been really upset about that. Me, too."

It didn't make sense after all. In the press room were stationed dozens of reporters from city papers around the U.S. Still, most of those papers only ran back-page stories about the flight.

"There's a lot going on in the world." T.J. explained that on top of the steel workers' strike and the British king's wedding, which were of great interest to Americans, there was a nasty civil war in Spain. Added to that, President Roosevelt was trying to pack three more justices into the Supreme Court.

"Why's that important?" Andrew asked.

"Because nine is the set number. The president wants additional judges who will support his economic programs."

"That's a little hard for me to understand," Ben said.

"The point is," T.J. said, "the world is a rocky place just now. Most people are interested in Amelia Earhart, but they think what she's doing is just for fun and not really important."

"Amelia Earhart is such a hero!" Lindsey said dreamily. "If they only knew."

"Yes, but they can't, so be sure you keep quiet about what you know," T.J. said firmly.

Chapter Eleven

Lindsey felt like a daffodil after an unexpected spring snow. The flower rejoices that it's spring, but it's weighed down by the chilling snow. One part of her gloried in Amelia Earhart's daring adventure. The other dreaded the part still to come—her hero's disappearance. And when would it happen? There certainly weren't any history books to consult. T.J. probably knew, but he was so busy that Lindsey couldn't get him alone to ask. The wait was terrible.

"It's like watching a disaster movie for the second time," Ben said. "You know what's coming, and you want to tell everyone so they'll get to safety."

"Couldn't we warn Amelia?" Lindsey asked on a sudden impulse. "Maybe we can let her know, and this will never happen!" Her face flushed with excitement.

"Sorry, Lindsey," Andrew said quietly. "Remember what T.J. says?"

Her shoulders slumped as Ben said, "We can only watch history happen. We can't change it."

"For once, I wish T.J. was wrong."

From June 7 until the end of the month Lindsey tracked Amelia Earhart's progress through Walter McMenamy and T.J., who continued traveling back and forth from L.A. to San Francisco. During that time, the aviatrix and Fred Noonan flew from the west coast of Africa all the way to Southeast Asia. Along the way they encountered bed bugs in the often strange places they stayed each night, terrible or non-existent sanitation, unknown foods that aggravated Amelia's stomach, and torrid heat.

At one African airport, such as it was, she and Noonan couldn't take off until the evening because of the heat. They couldn't refuel the Electra as they'd run the risk of the gasoline igniting on the searing metal of the plane.

The adventurers also faced tornadoes and sandstorms in Africa. Lindsey remembered Amelia's one fear—of crash landing on that continent, and so she prayed for her hero's safety. She guessed this prayer was okay, that it wasn't influencing history. As far as Lindsey could remember, Amelia and Fred Noonan made it across Africa.

Lord, I don't really know how to pray, she told God. *Her course is already determined, and you won't change it. I guess I should instead focus on her salvation. She simply can't go down without knowing you, and I'm not convinced she does.*

The flight didn't get easier once Amelia passed over Africa and on to the Middle East and Asia. Then on June 17, as Lindsey and the boys stood next to T.J. in the transmitting station, something happened. Lindsey couldn't tell what, as she didn't understand all the signals. The screen simply looked different, and T.J. looked nervous.

"What's happening, T.J.?" Lindsey shook his arm.

He hesitated, then said, "Amelia and Noonan are in the middle of torrential rains. It's the monsoon season."

"Where are they?" Andrew asked.

"They've just left Burma."

"Why didn't she go from east to west like the first time?" Walter McMenamy asked.

Lindsey walked over to him. "What do you mean?"

He looked startled. Apparently he'd been thinking out loud.

"She said they were going west to east this time because the weather would be more favorable," Lindsey said.

McMenamy's eyes wandered to the navy official standing tensely near T.J., waiting for more news.

"It hasn't been favorable since Africa," Ben commented.

"Of course it hasn't." McMenamy seemed angry. "Everyone knows it's the worst time of year in that region. She's going to face strong headwinds from now on, something that wouldn't have happened on the other route."

"Oh no!" T.J.'s face went white.

"What?" everyone shouted and quickly gathered around T.J.

"I've lost contact."

"You what?" the navy official asked nervously.

"Walter, see if you can pick up anything."

He couldn't. No one could. Several strained hours passed. Lindsey wondered if this was the day she dreaded. It wasn't, though. Radio communication was finally restored, and Amelia told T.J. that a bolt of lightning had struck the Electra, temporarily knocking out the radio. Everyone breathed more easily, and no one ever told the press what had happened.

Lindsey later learned that the rains were so severe they had knocked off patches of the Electra's paint. Amelia Earhart had been in real danger when she quickly retreated over the Bay of Bengal to avoid crashing into low-lying inland hills. She had to fly low, which left her and Noonan vulnerable to being swallowed whole by the merciless waves.

For the next week Amelia battled Asian monsoons. T.J. reported that she was exhausted and would be making a three-day stop at Bandoeng in what was then the Dutch East Indies. Three days turned into seven, however.

"The plane is rather tired, too," a navy official said. "It will be overhauled. T.J., you go home and get some rest, too."

At last Lindsey could ask T.J. all the questions about the flight that churned in her mind like butter. As they all walked out together, Walter McMenamy gave them all even more reason for worry.

"The plane doesn't need to be overhauled, T.J.," he said in a hushed tone.

"No?"

"Not at all. Of all the problems she's faced, including the plane's vibrations upsetting Noonan's navigational equipment, the engines have been fine. That plane only requires an oil change and normal inspection every fifty hours of flying time. Those engines are brand new, and she hasn't had any problems with them."

"What's going on then?" Andrew asked boldly.

"Maybe she just needs the rest," Lindsey suggested.

T.J. sighed. "Some things are better left unsaid, Walter." He put a hand on the man's shoulder.

"Okay, so there are some things I'm not supposed to know," he said. "Just tell me one thing, though. Is Amelia at peace about whatever she's doing?"

"Yes, she is."

"That's all I need to know."

But Lindsey wanted to know more. She decided to take advantage of this break in the action, and so she and the boys approached T.J. in his room that night.

"With all this cloak-and-dagger stuff going on," she began, "I'm wondering if Amelia really is resting at this place whose name I can't pronounce."

"Bandoeng," T.J. said.

"Yeah, that's the place."

T.J. was strangely quiet, and Lindsey was afraid he wouldn't address the question.

"Please," she said, clasping her hands together in a begging gesture.

T.J. laughed. "How can I resist? I forget that I don't have to keep secrets from y'all."

"No, you don't," Andrew said eagerly.

"But y'all have to keep these secrets," he ordered. "Not a word to anyone."

They promised to keep quiet.

"Good. Because if I hear a peep, I won't allow you to go to the station anymore."

"Not a peep," Lindsey and the boys said in unison.

T.J. took a deep breath. "Amelia *is* getting some rest, but they're also inspecting the special camera equipment they plan to use to photograph Japanese activity."

"On the 10-E?" Lindsey asked, referring to the plane.

"No, on the 12."

"The 12!" she exclaimed.

"What do you mean?" Ben asked.

"Yeah, the papers say the plane is a Lockheed Electra 10-E," Andrew said carefully, making sure he pronounced each word just right.

"That's what the government wants the public to think," T.J. explained. "Everyone thinks that the plane she crashed in Hawaii on her first around-the-world try was completely overhauled, that she's flying it now."

"But she's not?" Lindsey asked, shaking her head.

"No. That would've cost money the Putnams—G.P. and Amelia—didn't have, as I told you earlier. In addition, the government wants Amelia to have the top-of-the-line plane for her mission, and the 12 is more advanced than the 10-E."

Lindsey snapped her fingers. "That's it! That explains why the first time I saw the Electra it didn't have any markings on it. But right before Amelia went to Oakland for her test run, I saw identification numbers on it."

"Good observation, Lindsey!" T.J. patted her on the back. "You're right. The 10-E's ID numbers were painted on the 12 to make it look like the same plane."

"Is that why the press didn't get to see the plane up close?" Andrew asked.

"That's right," T.J. said. "It was also so they didn't see the camera equipment the government had installed."

"She is so brave," Lindsey said slowly, in admiration. "She's putting up with so much for her country."

Ben sniffed. "That may be true, but there's a lot of lying going on here. I don't like that part."

Lindsey wished he hadn't said that. She didn't like thinking her hero was involved in something deceptive. "It's not like that, Ben," she said. "She's putting her life on the line for her country, and certain things have to be kept secret for it to work."

Ben frowned. "You think Amelia Earhart can do no wrong."

"Well, I, uh…"

"Lindsey, I know you admire her, but she's just a human being," Ben said. "She has faults, too."

"I hardly call serving your country a fault," she argued.

No one said anything more, and Lindsey felt squirmy inside. She'd never fought with her cousin before. It didn't feel right.

"The suspense of knowing she's going to disappear but not knowing when is killing me," she said finally, breaking the silence. "Do you know when?" She leaned toward T.J.

"I don't know the exact time, but I know it will be within the next few days."

"Where will it happen?" Lindsey asked.

"It will be on her way from Lae, New Guinea, to a place called Howland Island," he said. "It's really stretching things to call it an island at all. It's actually a sandbar in the ocean called an atoll. Howland is only two miles long and three-quarters of a mile wide."

"How will she ever find it?" Ben asked incredulously.

"That's right," Andrew agreed. "Fred Noonan's natigal equipment isn't working right."

"Navigational, Andrew," Lindsey said matter-of-factly.

He shrugged. "Whatever. It's been giving him trouble."

"Yes, it has," T.J. said.

"Why in the world did she decide to land there of all places?" But Lindsey thought she knew the answer.

"That she was landing there gave our government the excuse to build a landing strip. The public is being told that it's to scope out Howland's possible use as an emergency landing site for Pacific commercial flights."

"But that's not it, right?" Lindsey asked. "It's because Howland Island is a good place for the United States to spy on the Japanese."

T.J. nodded.

"And so our ships can be there right now, near Japanese activity," Ben said, "because they can say they're receiving and giving signals to Amelia Earhart."

T.J. nodded his approval. "Y'all are really quick. I couldn't have explained things better myself."

"So, T.J., will Amelia find Howard Island?"

"No, Andrew, she won't find Howland Island."

"And no one will find her," Ben added darkly.

Chapter Twelve

Every night sound, even an owl's gentle hoots somewhere outside the window, crashed in Lindsey's ears like the engine of a plane starting up. Her body felt heavy, too. She couldn't find a comfortable position and continually switched from her side to her back to her stomach. To no avail. Lindsey could not fall asleep. Her mind whizzed and darted all over the place.

Maybe if I play an alphabet game, she thought. *Start with A, and recall all the names that begin with that letter. Andrew. Art. Audrey. Amos. Anne. Agatha. Amelia. Amelia. Amelia...*

In her dreams Lindsey and Amelia Earhart soared over the Hollywood sign in a canary yellow hot-air balloon. They climbed higher and higher until clouds swirled around their heads. Joy radiated from Amelia's weathered face. But Lindsey's own delight turned to sudden fear when a bee the size of a man's fist punctured the balloon with its stinger. As the craft veered wildly, Lindsey prayed, "Oh, God, please help us!" But Amelia Earhart's blissful expression did not change—she was flying, and that's all that seemed to matter.

Lindsey grasped the sides of the balloon's basket. How many minutes would pass before they crashed? Would she live through the impact, die, or time travel? Would she wake up in her Williamsburg, Virginia, home, Amelia's house, or heaven?

"Lindsey!" someone called.

"Where are you?" she asked.

"Lindsey?"

"Oh, please!"

Suddenly her eyelids popped open, and Lindsey looked into Mrs. DeCarrie's face as the woman stood over her. She quickly felt the sheets and covers and noted that her head was resting against a down pillow. A pinkish light shown through the window. Its reflection on the comforter was like a Monet painting. There was no hot air balloon and no Amelia Earhart. The clock on Lindsey's night table read six-thirty. It dawned on Lindsey—she'd been dreaming, of course.

Unfortunately, Mrs. DeCarrie wasn't in the least reassuring. Her reddened eyes and puffy cheeks made it obvious that she'd been crying. This wasn't turning out like it did at home whenever Lindsey awakened yelling from a nightmare. Her mother would always stroke her hair, saying, "Everything's all right, Lindsey. It was only a dream...."

This time everything clearly wasn't all right.

"Wh-what is it, Mrs. DeCarrie?"

"Lindsey, your father called." Her voice trembled. "Please get dressed right away. Then quickly pack your clothes and other belongings, and take them to the front door. My daughter will meet you there."

Still in a cloud of sleep, Lindsey wondered how in the world her father had spoken to Mrs. DeCarrie. Oh, her *father*! T.J.! But why had he called and from where? What was going on?

"What about the boys?" Lindsey asked, sitting up in bed.

"I've already awakened them," Mrs. DeCarrie said. "They're getting ready to leave."

"Wh-where are we going?" Lindsey swung her legs over the side of the twin bed.

"Your father wants you with him at the radio transmitting station," she said. Mrs. DeCarrie went to the closet and pulled out a brown Amelia Earhart suitcase. "I'll get you started in here. Please wash up and dress quickly." She yanked open the dresser drawers and began to pack Lindsey's clothes.

Maybe this was it, the time when Amelia Earhart would finally disappear. Why else would Mrs. DeCarrie be so upset, and why would Lindsey and the boys have to leave so suddenly? It was likely that T.J. wanted them all to be together because the mystery was about to be solved. The Dreamers would have to be ready to go home quickly. But where was T.J.?

"Is there something wrong with Amelia or the plane?" Lindsey asked.

The housekeeper stopped in the middle of sorting underwear. "I-I can't say for sure."

Was it because she didn't know or because she didn't want to say?

"We need to pray for Amelia, Mrs. DeCarrie," Lindsey said as she reached for her toothbrush. "Pray that God is watching over her and Fred Noonan."

"Yes, of course. Now please hurry, dear. My daughter is waiting."

Margot DeCarrie and the boys were standing in the entryway when Lindsey hurried downstairs. Everyone's eyes were still heavy with sleep, and they all exchanged strained good-mornings. In the garage sat Amelia's beautiful convertible, but Margot packed the children into a more ordinary sedan. On the roadways at that hour there was little traffic.

Lindsey felt like this was all still a bad dream. Since no one else was talking, she started to pray for Amelia and Fred Noonan. When they arrived at the radio station, they headed immediately to the transmitting room and paused outside. A press conference was going on down the hall. Lindsey listened as a flock of reporters squawked questions at someone.

"What are you hearing from her?" a deep male voice called out.

"Is she missing?" asked a female journalist.

"Come, children," Margot said.

"Just a second," Lindsey pleaded.

"No, Amelia Earhart is not missing," Lieutenant Williams said in response to the questions. "The Coast Guard cutter *Itasca* has been unable to make contact with the Electra, however."

"Is she near Howland Island?" someone asked.

"We aren't sure at this point, but every effort is being made to locate her."

"How much fuel does she have left?" the same female reporter wanted to know.

At first Williams didn't respond, then he said, "We're concerned about that."

"Let's go, Lindsey," Margot DeCarrie said.

They entered the smoke-filled transmitting room where long faces and worry lines were in abundance. T.J. removed his headphones when he saw his "family" and rose quietly to greet them. His tightly drawn lips and frown lines told Lindsey that the time of Amelia's disappearance had come.

"Thanks for bringing them, Margot," he said.

"That's all right." Tears had formed in Margot's dark eyes. "We could have kept them at the house, you know."

T.J. shook his head. "Thank you for offering, but it's just best to have them with me right now. Besides, your hands will be full once the rest of the news world wakes up to this story."

"What's happening?" Margot asked, shredding a paper tissue in her hands. "Did they crash when they left Lae? I knew they would be heavier than usual carrying that fuel for the next leg of the flight."

"They didn't crash, Margot, but Amelia did have some trouble taking off early this morning our time. You're right. The plane was quite heavy."

As T.J. spoke, Lindsey noticed Walter McMenamy sitting on the opposite side of the room. He was speaking into a microphone and looked both worried and frustrated. She caught his eye, and they nodded somberly at each other.

"But they were all right?" Margot asked. "They got off the ground?"

"It was pretty hair-raising, but yes, they made it up."

"Where are they now?" Ben asked as some navy officials began to scurry around the room like frightened mice.

"That's the problem. We don't know. Amelia hasn't been transmitting very much, but they're either headed into or now in the middle of a nasty squall line."

"What's that?" Andrew asked.

Lindsey tried to concentrate on T.J.'s words, but the flurry of activity and noise among the handful of people in the room kept distracting her.

"A squall is a type of strong thunderstorm activity," he said.

"When was the last you heard from her?" Margot asked. "I want to give Mother and Mrs. Earhart as much news as I possibly can. They'll want to know."

"Of course," T.J. said. "We heard from her a couple of hours ago. But the *Itasca's* radio operators can't get a fix on her direction. Apparently Amelia's having trouble finding Howland Island."

Margot sighed. "We were so afraid of that." She paused for a moment, then asked, "Where's G.P.?"

"At the Beacon Hill station in San Francisco. We're keeping in fairly constant contact with him."

Margot seemed to hesitate before taking her leave. Finally she asked, "T.J., do you think everything will be all right?"

Lindsey couldn't watch. No, everything wasn't going to be all right.

"I...I'm afraid I can't tell you right now," T.J. stammered, "but I'll keep in touch."

Margot sighed. "I guess I'd better go and tell Mrs. Earhart before she hears the news on the radio. T.J., please call me as soon as you know something." She grasped T.J.'s hand for a moment, then headed for the door.

T.J. turned to Lindsey and the boys. "Come with me," he said.

They followed him to a private room off the radio transmission center. It was dusty, and after Lindsey sneezed twice, she focused her attention on T.J.'s update.

"What's really going on?" Andrew asked.

"Amelia has been very careful about letting us know exactly where she is," T.J. said. "She and Noonan can get a precise bearing if they need to."

"Why don't they then?" Lindsey wanted to know.

"Well, because they've been flying over enemy territory."

"Japanese?" she asked. "So she's doing the spy thing now?"

T.J. nodded. "We don't want the Japanese in the area to get a fix on the Electra."

"Does getting a fix mean finding out where they are?" Ben asked.

"That's right." T.J. lowered his voice. "Back then our country didn't know just how advanced Japanese tracking systems were. Actually their equipment was far better than anything we had at the time."

"But have the Japanese actually picked up Amelia's signals?" Lindsey asked.

T.J. inhaled deeply. "I'm afraid so. G.P. telegraphed me fifteen minutes ago. According to him, Amelia's trying to dodge the Japanese, who are on military maneuvers in that area. She and Noonan have even been fired at a couple of times."

"Oh, wow!" Lindsey wasn't expecting to hear this bit of news. "They haven't been hit, have they?"

"No. Amelia is giving radio signals that she hopes the *Itasca* will figure out just in case the ship needs to rescue her. It's confusing to the radio operators on board the ship, though. You see, many of Amelia's signals have to be unclear in order to deceive the Japanese."

"So, has she been able to photograph Japanese activity?" Lindsey asked.

"Yes, the cameras on the Electra are running."

"She is such a hero!" Lindsey exclaimed. "To think she's putting her life on the line like this for her country."

"Don't overdo it, Lindsey," Andrew said.

"Overdo it!" she cried. "How can I overdo it when she's so courageous?"

"Listen up, folks," T.J. interrupted them. "I need to have

you nearby because this mystery is close to getting solved. At the same time, you must be on your best behavior. Understood?"

They all nodded. "Understood," they repeated, though out of sync.

Lindsey and the boys returned to the main transmitting room and sat quietly as T.J. went back to work. Tense energy pulsed through the place like a rapid heartbeat. Lindsey sat on the edge of her chair, waiting for news of further radio signals from Amelia.

Finally, at 8:47 A.M. T.J. cried, "I have something!" Everyone crowded around as he slowly repeated Amelia's words, "We are in line of position 157-337. Will repeat this message on 6210 KC. Wait. Listening on 6210. We are running north and south."

"Did you actually hear her voice?" Lindsey asked as everyone began to mutter around her.

"The *Itasca* received the message at 8:44 and just relayed it to us," he said.

"How did she sound?" Walter McMenamy asked.

"Anxious, I'm afraid."

T.J. was soon so swamped with questions that Lindsey and the boys returned to their seats. She started biting her nails.

"Will you stop that?" Andrew asked.

"Sorry, I'll try," she promised. She began wiggling her right foot.

"Lind-sey."

"Look, Andrew, I can either bite my nails or swing my foot. Take your pick. I'm nervous."

"Bite your nails," he said.

At a little after nine, T.J. announced, "I have something else."

Once again, everyone crowded around him.

"A radio operator west of Howland Island picked her up," he said. "He heard Amelia say, 'Land in sight ahead.'"

Just then Lieutenant Williams pressed through the group and tapped T.J. on the shoulder. "Will everyone excuse us for a minute, please?" he asked, frowning darkly at the Dreamers.

Lindsey guessed he didn't appreciate their presence.

"McMenamy," Williams said, "stay here please."

The lieutenant huddled in heated discussion with T.J. and Walter McMenamy. Lindsey could hear Walter disagreeing with Lieutenant Williams. He calmed down, though, when Williams said, "Amelia would want it this way."

The next thing Lindsey knew the officer was outside in the hall calling a press conference. The group of reporters and photographers seemed to have multiplied, and they followed Williams into the press area. Lindsey and the boys slipped out of the radio transmission room to listen.

"Ladies and gentlemen!" A number of them were still talking, though, so Williams repeated himself. "Ladies and gentlemen, a massive search is underway for Amelia Earhart and her navigator, Fred Noonan."

The press gave a collective gasp. From her position on the fringe of the crowd, Lindsey saw their shocked faces.

"It is the largest sea-and-air search in history," he said. The hall lit up with flashbulbs, and reporters quickly scratched notes on their tablets. "We are making every effort to find them."

"When did you last hear from Amelia?" someone called out.

"At 8:44," Williams answered.

Lindsey and the boys gaped at each other. That was a lie.

"Was she near Howland Island?"

"We are assuming that she was," Williams said.

"How much fuel does she have left?" another reporter asked.

"We are assuming that her fuel supply has been exhausted."

Lindsey motioned Andrew and Ben to come closer. "Lieutenant Williams is lying through his teeth," she hissed.

Chapter Thirteen

After the press conference T.J. took Lindsey and the boys aside. Lines of weariness traced his green eyes. His reddish blond hair was almost as rumpled as Amelia Earhart's usually was.

"I just spoke with G.P. up at the Coast Guard station in San Francisco," he said.

"What did he say?" Lindsey asked.

"He wants me to go up there immediately."

"But you can't!" Ben kept his voice to a low roar. "We have to stay together or we won't get back. You know that."

"And the mystery's almost over, so it would be too dangerous for us be apart," Lindsey said.

T.J. pumped his open hands downward a few times, directing them to be quiet. "Y'all are going with me," he said.

Lindsey let out a soft, "Phew!" and passed the back of her hand over her forehead.

"G.P. doesn't know y'all are coming, though, and he might not be entirely pleased about it. Nevertheless, we need to stay together."

"How will we get there?" Andrew asked.

"Paul Mantz is going to fly us in one of his planes. Just like he's been flying me back and forth all along." T.J. sighed, made a face, and gripped his stomach.

They left Burbank at ten o'clock that morning and arrived

in San Francisco in time for a late lunch. A Coast Guard limousine picked them up, then quickly shuttled them to the Beacon Hill station where G.P. waited with the few officials who knew the true nature of Amelia's quest.

T.J. and G.P. started to shake hands, then awkwardly embraced instead. Lindsey caught Putnam's eye as he looked over T.J.'s shoulder. He gaped at her and the boys.

"T.J.," he said, breaking away, "I didn't know you'd be bringing the kids. I just assumed they'd stay at the house."

T.J. explained quietly about Lindsey's nightmares. "I wanted to keep her and the boys nearby. I'm sure there's a place here where they can stay. I assure you, they won't be a problem."

"Of course," G.P. said. Then he announced, "T.J., kids, I'd like you to meet Lieutenant Fischer, who's been on the radio with me up here. Fischer, this is T.J. Wakesnoris, Amelia's radio advisor, and his children, Lindsey, Ben, and Andrew." G.P. paused for a moment, then asked, "So, Fischer, where can the kids stay? They need to be close to their dad."

The squat man with a huge bald spot on the top of his head thought about that. "There's a supply room down the hall with a few cots and a radio," he said. "It's not much, but at least they'll be out of the...uh...they'll be comfortable."

"I'll take them there and be right back," T.J. said.

"I'll show you the way," Fischer offered.

The room was about the size of Lindsey's bedroom back in Williamsburg. It had four cots, reserved for officers on duty, and a metal table upon which sat a lamp, radio, and a Gideon Bible. Lindsey saw a tiny broom closet in one corner. The room's single window looked out over the city stretching out to the cold gray Pacific Ocean.

"I'll have some lunch sent down from the mess hall," Lieutenant Fischer said.

This took next to no time at all. The Dreamers were soon settled in with warm bottles of Coke and toasted tuna fish sandwiches.

"The room's not much," Lindsey said, "but that view makes it worth more than a night at the Williamsburg Inn."

"Yeah, and T.J.'s right down the hall for when it's time to go home," Ben said.

"Let's just hope he comes here to lie down if he gets sleepy." Andrew sounded skeptical.

After lunch they laid on the cots and listened to radio reports about Amelia Earhart. There were continual updates throughout the day, which helped pass the time.

"They didn't give her this much coverage before," Lindsey grumbled, and the boys agreed.

The various radio stations announced the same news— that Amelia Earhart and Fred Noonan were last heard from at 8:44 A.M. That they would have run out of fuel within a half hour. That a massive search and rescue effort was underway involving four thousand men, ten ships, and sixty-five planes. These covered a quarter of a million square miles in the Pacific Ocean.

T.J. heard differently on his exclusive hook-up. Each night for the next three weeks he filled the Dreamers in on the real story before they went to sleep. They learned that Amelia's signals did not end on July 2 at 8:44 A.M. Instead she continued to send transmissions for the next several days. The navy, however, quickly discredited those reports as frauds when rumors reached the press.

"It's very important for the government to let the public think Amelia's plane went down somewhere in the ocean," T.J. told Lindsey and the boys. "That way the spy mission part of her journey will never be known. In the 1930s Americans would have been devastated to find out the president had lied to them."

In addition, T.J. learned that Amelia and Noonan actually had been shot down by a Japanese pilot. With one damaged wing, the Electra crash-landed on an uncharted sandspit north of the Gilbert Islands. The Japanese had the only ships in that region, and they took their time finding the Americans.

Amelia had continued broadcasting signals until her radio's power supply drained. Just before that happened, she reported the arrival of a Japanese cruiser. In her final message on July 5 she said, "He must be at least an admiral."

"So she was captured!" Lindsey exclaimed.

"What happened to Fred Noonan?" asked Andrew. "Was he captured, too?"

"We're not entirely sure," T.J. said. "Amelia reported that Noonan was injured in the crash, but we aren't sure how badly he was hurt."

For a long moment the only sound was city noise outside the window.

"I don't see why the navy couldn't have rescued them," Andrew said finally. "If they knew what happened, they should have tried to help."

T.J. looked him in the eye. "That would've been nice, Andrew, but it wasn't a possibility. When Amelia agreed to this mission, she knew that if anything went wrong, that would be it. She'd be on her own. That's how the spy game works, I'm afraid."

"That's horrible," Lindsey said. "And yet," she brightened, "that's just the kind of person she is. So brave and daring and patriotic."

"I guess it's time to go home, then," Ben said. "I sure am ready after sleeping on this cot for three weeks." He poked the lumpy mattress.

"Maybe it's not time yet." Lindsey pursed her lips. She stroked the scarf Amelia had given her, the one she had worn every day since her hero's adventure had begun. "What happened to Amelia after she was captured, T.J.? We don't know that yet, do we?"

"Well, what did happen?" Andrew asked.

T.J. shook his head. "I have no idea."

On July 19 the Navy issued a statement. The search for Amelia Earhart had been called off. T.J. told the Dreamers in private shortly before the official announcement was made.

"G.P. just left for home," he said. "He went back to arrange a memorial service for Amelia."

"You mean she's dead?" Andrew asked.

"As far as we know, she isn't," T.J. said. "However, the public will be told that she and Fred Noonan drowned when the plane ran out of fuel and went down somewhere near Howland Island."

"Arranging a service is going to seem pretty weird for G.P., isn't it?" Lindsey asked. "I mean, since he knows Amelia's really alive and all."

"That's true, but G.P. is choosing to go along with the official statement," T.J. said.

"That poor man." Lindsey could feel herself starting to cry. "This must be really hard on him. Will he ever know?"

"I'm not sure, Lindsey."

"Will we?" Ben asked.

"Yes, I have a feeling we will."

"But how?"

"At this point, Ben, only the Lord knows. We must once again trust that he has everything under control."

On July 21 Lindsey was among hundreds of others who gathered in Hollywood's Episcopal church for a memorial service honoring Amelia Earhart. Wearing a dress and the scarf Amelia had given her, Lindsey sat between Walter McMenamy and T.J. in the third row. The boys sat to their teacher's right. As she waited for the service to begin, Lindsey scanned the church's stained glass windows that stretched from the sanctuary's floor to its arched ceiling. It was raining outside, though, which made it hard for Lindsey to see the themes each window portrayed.

An elderly, silver-haired pastor in a black robe stepped to the pulpit. People stopped talking to their neighbors and turned their attention to the front of the church.

"Welcome to this service for our beloved wife, daughter, and sister, Amelia," the pastor began. His voice sounded surprisingly high and young for someone as old as Lindsey figured he must be—at least seventy. "Jesus said, 'I am the resurrection and the life. He that believes in me, though he die, shall yet live. And whoever lives and believes in me shall never die.' Let us pray."

Lindsey bowed her head and closed her eyes. Did Amelia believe in Jesus? And what about Fred Noonan? If only the answers were yes.

The minister began to pray, "Eternal God, our heavenly Father, you love us with an everlasting love and can turn the shadow of death into the morning. Help us to wait upon you with reverent and believing hearts. In the silence of this hour, speak to us of eternal things. Give us hope through the comfort of your Scriptures, and lift us above our darkness and distress to the light and peace of Jesus Christ our Lord, in whose name we pray. Amen."

A chorous of "Amens" flowed through the church.

"Let us worship God by turning to hymn number 521," the pastor announced.

T.J. plucked a hymnbook from the pew rack and thumbed his way to "Eternal Father, Strong to Save." He motioned to Lindsey that he would share with her, and she held her end of the book. Two pews ahead, Amelia Earhart's sister helped their mother locate the hymn in the book. What must they be going through?

Lindsey had trouble getting through the song. She kept choking up. The congregation completed the majestic hymn about God's presence in times of peril, then sat down.

"Hear these words of comfort from the holy Scriptures," the pastor said. "First, from Psalm 23. 'The Lord is my shepherd, I shall not want....'"

He read several more passages, and then a stately woman rose and sang "O God, Our Help in Ages Past." She carried herself in the self-assured manner of a celebrity, but Lindsey didn't recognize her. This was, after all, way before her time.

"We will now hear from several of Amelia's closest friends and relatives as they eulogize our dear sister," the pastor announced when the singing had ended.

Andrew turned to Ben. "What's a youlgy?"

"When people say nice things about someone who died."

The first came from Paul Mantz, Amelia's long-time flying instructor and pal. With shining eyes the handsome pilot told a few stories about her courage. Lindsey especially liked the one in which her hero had narrowly avoided drowning.

"Amelia would fly anything that had wings," Mantz said. "Back in '33 she took a Keystone Loening Air Yacht on its maiden flight from Cleveland to Detroit. When the fog became thick as pea soup, Amelia landed the amphibious plane right onto Lake Erie. She and her copilot bobbed like ducks on five-foot waves. The plane was not equipped with a radio, so they couldn't tell anyone where they were. When the fog finally lifted three hours later, Amelia took the plane right to Detroit as planned. She thought the whole thing was 'a great lark.'"

Gentle laughter rippled through the congregation. Lindsey liked remembering Amelia this way.

"Amelia, you're a woman of the ages." Mantz's voice cracked as he finished his speech. "And a hero for all time."

The minister stepped to the lectern. "We will now hear from one of Amelia's devoted advisors, Mr. Thomas Jefferson Wakesnoris."

Lindsey smiled bravely at T.J. Then she gasped. He had fallen asleep!

"T.J.!" she whispered urgently. "T.J., wake up! It's your turn."

She and Andrew started to shake him gently as uneasy

murmurs spread through the congregation.

"C'mon, T.J." But Andrew's coaxing wasn't working.

Ben reached around Andrew to jolt his teacher awake. Just then Lindsey felt the familiar time travel sensation—the tingling in her hand where she touched T.J. The feeling swept quickly throughout her body.

"Andrew," she said, "do you feel it?"

"Yeah. Hang on, guys."

The last thing Lindsey heard was the minister coughing nervously into the microphone.

Chapter Fourteen

When Lindsey emerged from her time travel wooziness, she expected to find herself on a 747 plane bound for Hawaii. But as her eyes adjusted to her surroundings, she sat up in shock. She was sitting on a straw-covered dirt floor and wearing a filthy overall that was stiff where mud had hardened the thin material. Once upon a long time ago the outfit had been dark green. Now it was faded and smelled sour. The room itself reeked. It reminded Lindsey of a litter box that someone had neglected to empty for a month.

A fly the size of a nickel buzzed around her badly matted hair. She swatted it angrily with her sore right hand. That poor hand always hurt after time traveling!

Lindsey shivered from dampness and fear. Feeble sunlight wandered half-heartedly into the room through a barred window way above her head. This had to be a jail cell.

Her eyes fell upon four figures at the other end of the room, which was about the size of a large kitchen. She tried to stand only to find herself wobbling like a newborn colt. Instead Lindsey crawled through maggot-infested straw to the other side. She felt queasy from the filth.

T.J., Ben, and Andrew were just beginning to stir. Lindsey couldn't tell who the fourth person was, but the figure was all curled up in a fetal position.

"Lindsey," T.J. said weakly, "is that you?"

"Yes, it's me." She started to lean against the wall, but then saw how slimy it was. She drew back quickly with a shudder.

"Where are we?" Ben mumbled as he awakened.

Andrew wrinkled his nose. "Wherever it is, it sure smells bad."

"I thought we time traveled," Ben said.

"We did," Lindsey said with a frown. "I think. Why aren't we on the plane going to Hawaii, T.J.?"

"If this is Hawaii, we're in big trouble," Ben said. "These clothes are vile!"

All of them wore the same type of overall, and they all smelled like a cesspool.

T.J. sat up and looked around the room as he brushed straw from his clothes. "Who's that, Lindsey?" He pointed to the silent figure.

"I don't know. I was just about to ask you."

"I'll check it out in a minute." He stretched, then asked, "Is everyone all right?"

"Sort of," Andrew said. "This place is creeping me right out."

"Same here." Ben nodded. "Th-this is weird, T.J."

"Why aren't we in our own time again?" Andrew asked. "What happened when we left the church?"

Lindsey had an idea. "Although we've never time traveled twice for the same adventure, I think that's what happened here. We should've gone right back to where we started from, but we went someplace else instead." She shook her head in confusion. "Are we further back in time than 1937?"

Just then they heard high-pitched male voices beyond the door. Foreign voices. One of the men shook the door, shouted something at them, then went away.

"I think we're in a prison somewhere," T.J. said.

"Prison!" Ben shouted. "What does that have to do with Amelia Earhart? Aren't we ever going to get home?"

Lindsey wondered that herself.

"Now, Ben, I can tell you're scared, but I'm sure the Lord has this under control," T.J. said. "He's never let us down before, has he?" He paused. "I'm beginning to put two and two together here. When we left Amelia's memorial service, none of us knew what ultimately had happened to her after she was captured. The mystery wasn't fully solved."

Lindsey suddenly felt more hopeful. "You're right! We're not home because we don't know the solution to the mystery yet."

"So, we're not stuck in time?" Ben asked.

"I don't think so," T.J. said.

"Look!" Lindsey pointed to the still-unidentified person who was now stirring.

Very hesitantly she inched her way toward the crumpled figure. The person had started to sit up, then fell back exhausted, moaning in pain. Lindsey moved closer, and T.J. was immediately at her side. The boys followed.

"Wat-er," the person said.

"Andrew, Ben, see if there's any water in here," T.J. said. "Here, let me help you sit up." As he assisted the person, T.J. said, "Lindsey, get some straw and tuck it behind him, will you?"

She quickly did as she was told. She noticed that the other prisoner was extremely thin and pale. His hair was long and matted like Lindsey's, only worse. She tried not to be overwhelmed by the person's awful odor, but it was tough. She had always been sensitive to smells.

"This was all we could find." Andrew held out a tin of stagnant water.

"This is gross," T.J. said. "But it's all we have."

T.J. lifted the cup to the prisoner's lips, and he drank thirstily. Afterwards, the stranger slumped against the straw, sitting semi-upright.

"Maybe he can tell us where we are," Andrew said.

"Let's talk to him." Lindsey moved closer to the figure. "Hi, I'm Lindsey Sk-uh Wakesnoris." She'd almost forgotten that she was still T.J.'s daughter. "What's your name?"

The prisoner's blue eyes suddenly opened wide. "Lindsey?"

The voice was that of a woman. Lindsey was momentarily speechless. "You know me?" she asked.

The prisoner nodded feebly.

"Who are you?"

"A-mel-ia."

"Amelia Earhart!" Lindsey screamed the name, which brought the guards rushing to the door. They all cowered as the jailers yelled in a language the Dreamers didn't understand.

"You're Amelia Earhart?" Andrew asked quietly after the men left.

She nodded weakly. "How-did-you-get-here?" She formed the words sluggishly but clearly.

T.J. took her emaciated hand in his. "Amelia, it's T.J. God sent us. He wants us to be with you so we can know what happened to you after you disappeared." He paused. "And so you won't be alone."

"T-J! Yes. God-has-sent-you." She spoke each word with great effort.

Lindsey's heart quickened. "Did you say 'God'?"

"He's been so good." She paused. "To me." Amelia reached under her jumpsuit and pulled out a battered cross.

"It's the one I gave you!" Lindsey was beside herself as Amelia smiled weakly.

"I'd hardly call this place good," Ben muttered to Andrew.

Amelia heard him and tugged at the boy's sleeve. "God's been so close—my strength," she said through paper-dry lips.

In spite of Amelia's smelly condition, Lindsey hugged her tightly.

"This must be the end of the mystery," T.J. said. "We've done something new this time, or should I say, God has done something new?"

"What?" Lindsey asked.

"He's taken us forward in time. God is showing us what happened after Amelia was captured."

"But where—and when—are we?" Andrew asked.

"Oh, I do hope she's strong enough to tell us," Lindsey said.

"I am. Come closer."

They gathered around, and Amelia told them her story, stopping and starting periodically to catch her breath.

After the Japanese plane had shot down the Electra, Amelia continued broadcasting until the batteries finally gave out. That was something the Dreamers already knew. What they didn't know, however, was that Fred Noonan had been seriously banged up in the crash. He had sustained a head wound and a nasty cut on his knee. On July 5, 1937, a Japanese destroyer picked them up and took them to the island of Saipan, which was then under Japanese occupation.

"They kept us there for a time—in a hotel," Amelia said. "We were prisoners." She coughed harshly and couldn't speak again for a few minutes. Her strength seemed to be almost gone.

"Maybe you should stop talking," Lindsey said, although she desperately wanted to know the whole story.

"No." Amelia shook her head. "Must go on. I haven't long."

Lindsey cried softly as she learned what had happened. The Japanese had kept Amelia and her navigator in Saipan for several months. Amelia couldn't remember the exact length of time. Then she and Noonan were put on a ship bound for Tokyo, but he died on the way. The cut on his knee was never properly treated, and an infection had developed that claimed his life.

The Japanese had tried to get Amelia to talk about U.S. activity in the South Pacific. They also wanted her to tell them how prepared for war the American military was. But Amelia had refused to say anything at all—even under torture. She was squirreled away in a Tokyo prison until the United States and Japan went to war against each other in December 1941.

"Why didn't the Japanese tell the Americans they had captured you?" Andrew wanted to know.

Amelia slowly explained that if the Japanese had done that, the United States would have demanded to know why their military vessels had been in that area of the Pacific in the first place.

"Remember, the Japanese had occupied many islands illegally," T.J. reminded the Dreamers. "They might have lost the empire they were building."

"So, why didn't President Roosevelt demand that Japan tell

us if they had Amelia?" Lindsey asked. "That would have given him a perfect excuse to expose what the Japanese were doing."

T.J. shook his head. "FDR would have had to admit that he had acted against the wishes of Congress and the American people by sending Amelia on a dangerous spy mission. The public might never have trusted him again, and Amelia's reputation would be ruined."

"But she's a hero!" Lindsey said.

"Not if she were caught spying for the U.S. government," T.J. said. "The American people were against interfering with other countries, remember?"

Amelia nodded in agreement. She slowly went on to explain that after the United States declared war against the Japanese, she was moved from prison to prison. She was held both in Japan and in China, which the Japanese then controlled.

"Where are we now?" Lindsey asked Amelia.

"China."

"Do you know what year it is?"

She nodded weakly. "July 1945."

Eight years after Amelia's disappearance!

"Was the war still going on then?" Lindsey asked T.J.

"Yes and no. Germany surrendered in April. In August the U.S. will drop atomic bombs on two Japanese cities. Then they'll surrender, and the war will be over."

"What will happen to Amelia?" Lindsey asked.

T.J. didn't respond. He didn't have to. At that moment Amelia raised her arms to heaven and smiled radiantly. Her thin, pale features looked young again. Once more Lindsey saw the Amelia she had first met in California in 1937, vibrant and alive. Except that now Amelia Earhart was even more alive than before because she had Christ in her heart. Her last word was, "Jesus."

Lindsey bent over her and cried for sadness and for joy. That Amelia had lived in peace as a prisoner for eight years was truly amazing. She looked up at T.J. "Nothing is impossible with God, is it?" she said through her tears.

Just then two guards started unlocking the door. T.J. went to see what they wanted. The men, dressed in Japanese uniforms, shoved him hard. Then one knocked T.J. to the floor with his rifle butt.

"No!" Lindsey cried out from Amelia's side.

The boys rushed over to T.J.

"He's unconscious," Ben said. "Andrew, do you feel that?"

"I sure do. Lindsey!" Andrew shouted across the cell. "Get over here. My hand is tingling. I think it's time to go home!"

"I'm going fast!" Ben said. "Hurry up, Lindsey!"

She squeezed Amelia's arm in farewell, then let go. She started scrambling across the straw-covered floor, but one of the jailers blocked her path. He laughed down at her harshly and kicked at her.

"Stop that! I have to get home."

Of course, the guard didn't understand her. He leered at her while his partner checked on Amelia's condition.

What would happen if Lindsey couldn't make it back to T.J.? The boys kept yelling at her to come until finally they were swallowed up in time. Would she die a prisoner as Amelia had? Would anyone at home ever miss her? Or in her own time, would she have lived at all? "Oh, Lord, please help me!" she cried. "I must get to them!"

The guard near Amelia said something to the one hovering over Lindsey. When she saw that he was momentarily distracted, she summoned all her strength and made a mad dash for T.J. The guard grabbed at her just as she slid into her teacher like a baseball player into home plate.

She grasped T.J.'s ankle and held on for dear life. The guard rushed over, however, and began pulling her away. "Please, Lord, help me hang on!" she gasped. Then she remembered a Bible verse she had learned in Sunday school. "'The name of the Lord is a strong tower. The righteous run to it and are safe.' Oh, God, please be my strong tower!"

Suddenly Lindsey felt as if she were being swallowed by a crashing wave. Then, just when she couldn't hold on to T.J. any longer, she blacked out.

The next thing Lindsey knew, she was sitting on a 747 next to her brother. When she saw where she was, she wept quietly with relief. "Thank you, Lord," she said. "Thank you."

"Are you all right?" Andrew asked as he stroked her arm gently. "You had us scared."

"We weren't sure you'd make it back," Ben said from across the aisle. "It was awful, wasn't it, T.J.?"

"Yes," he said, "but she did make it. God came to her rescue."

"I—I'm okay. Just a bit shaky." Lindsey smiled. "And my hand hurts."

"Mine, too!" the boys said in unison.

"Did we really go back to Amelia Earhart's time—back and forth, that is?" she asked. "Or was it all a dream?"

"Yes, Lindsey." T.J. smiled. "It was a dream—an impossible dream."